Solid Foundation Sermon Starters

2 CORINTHIANS

Blueprints for 30 messages built upon God's Word

Howard A. Hayes

Cincinnati, Ohio

Cover design by Grannan Graphic Design LTD

Interior design by Robert E. Korth

Edited by Jim Eichenberger

Printed in the U.S.A.

Solid Foundation™ is a trademark of
Standard Publishing, Cincinnati, Ohio.
A division of Standex International Corporation.
07 06 05 04 03 02 01 00 5 4 3 2 1

Contents

Introduction to 2 Corinthians

Various Passages

Second Corinthians might well be called a crisis epistle. It was written from Paul's stressful state of mind to deal with a number of problems in the Corinthian church. It was written from Macedonia during Paul's third missionary journey, probably in A.D. 57 or 58.

I. BACKGROUND OF THE LETTER

A. Paul had left Asia under the threat of death (1:8; Acts 19:23; 1 Corinthians 15:32; 16:9). Arriving in Troas he had expected to meet Titus with some word from Corinth; and even though the Lord had opened a door for Paul, he was so distressed in spirit that he left Troas and pressed on into Macedonia (2:12, 13).

B. Reaching Philippi he "had no rest" but was "troubled on every side; without were fightings, within were fears" (7:5). This anxiety and turmoil of spirit was not eased until he met Titus returning from Corinth with the good news that his former letter had been received graciously (7:6, 7), and that the church's attitude had changed from carelessness and obstinacy to repentance.

II. PROBLEMS PAUL NEEDED TO ADDRESS

A. In Corinth some were accusing him of fickleness because he had changed his plans to visit them (1:17ff).

B. There was need for a forgiving spirit toward an offending brother in the congregation (2:5-11).

C. Some were lacking in appreciation for the character and importance of the Christian ministry (2:14–6:10).

D. There was need for the separation of the church members from worldly entanglements (6:1–7:1).

E. There was urgency for completing the relief offering for the poor Judean Christians (8:1ff).

F. Some were questioning the validity of Paul's apostleship and ministry (10:1ff).

G. Paul needed to assure them of his love and concern despite his former "sharp" letter (2:3, 4; 7:8ff).

TEXTUAL HIGHLIGHTS

The church in Corinth provided cause for both thanksgiving (1 Corinthians 1:4) and anxiety (2 Corinthians 2:3-5). At this point, Paul's anxiety *is* great concerning his relationship with the church and the well-being of the cause which he loved so dearly. The main purpose of this letter was to vindicate Paul's apostleship and to protect the church from the inroads of false teachers. Many would label it as the most personal of all his epistles to a congregation, and it has been described as the impassioned self-defense of a wounded spirit to erring and ungrateful children. Because there is no central theological theme or logical progression in the epistle, it is difficult to make a well-ordered outline of it; but the apostle's genius for problem-solving is abundantly evident and has been beneficial to the church universal throughout her history.

ILLUSTRATIONS

Corinthian trouble again! Greek mythology tells the story of Sisyphus, son of Aeolus and founder and king of Corinth. The legend tells of this crafty king who tried to cheat the gods and death itself. For his arrogance, he was condemned to eternal punishment in Tartarus. There he eternally pushed a heavy rock to the top of a steep hill, where it would always roll down again, causing him to have to begin his struggle afresh.

Paul may have thought of this ancient story when dealing with the church at Corinth. Because of their arrogance and independence, the Corinthians seemed to face one crisis after another. Just as one problem seemed to be under control, everything would suddenly "go downhill" again!

Respect for authority. In 2 Corinthians Paul responds to those who would question his apostleship. Some in the church in Corinth argued that Paul had no right to tell them what to do. They did not respect his authority.

In March of 1999, Shell Oil Company commissioned a nationwide opinion poll on a variety of topics. The poll asked, "In the past ten years, have we gotten much stronger as a nation, somewhat stronger as a nation, somewhat weaker as a nation, or much weaker as a nation in terms of respect for authority?" Eighty-six percent of those responding rated attitudes as "somewhat weaker" or "much weaker." Lack of respect for authority is a problem of humankind throughout history, and one that shows no sign of lessening today.

God Comforts His People

2 Corinthians 1:3-11

Paul describes God as "the Father of mercies, and the God of all comfort" (v. 3). This description lays the foundation to the main themes of this epistle. Those themes outline the need for reconciliation and the need for a merciful attitude and mutual concern for each other.

The comfort of God is an encouraging assurance which runs all through the Bible. It has a twofold character: objective and subjective. Objectively, it is an expression of God's favor; subjectively, it is a manifestation of brotherly concern.

I. GOD COMFORTS US IN OUR AFFLICTIONS (v. 4).

A. The apostle is bold and confident in this declaration. His own personal experience "in Asia" (v. 8; Acts 19:23ff; 1 Corinthians 15:32; 16:9) gives weight to this affirmation. He knows from experience the mercy of God and is persuaded of its universal application for all who are committed to Him.

B. The corollary to this divine function is that God's people, the Christian community, are to exercise the same toward each other. By virtue of our identity with God through Christ we are enabled to administer grace. "We are ambassadors for Christ" (5:20).

C. God employs and appoints many agencies for this administration. He comforts us by His Word (Romans 15:4); by the Holy Spirit (Acts 5:32); by prophets (1 Corinthians 14:3, 31); by co-laborers (2 Corinthians 7:6); by Christian fellowship (1 Thessalonians 5:11); etc.

II. AFFLICTION AND PERSECUTION ARE REDEMPTIVE (vv. 5-7).

A. Affliction and persecution have a twofold effect—social and personal.

1. Just as Christ's sufferings "abound in us," they also motivate us to minister to others for their "consolation and salvation" (v. 6). Paul is confident of this persuasion (v. 7).
2. Afflictions enhance our personal growth. It has been said that trial, persecution, and suffering are the growth environment of the Christian. For this reason Paul could say, "We glory in tribulations also; knowing that tribulation worketh patience [perseverance]; and patience, experience; and experience, hope: and hope maketh not ashamed [does not disappoint us]" (Romans 5:3-5; James 1:2).

B. Later in this letter Paul emphasized this truth further: "Our light affliction, which is but for a moment, worketh for us a far more exceeding and eternal weight of glory" (4:17). The Hebrew writer comments upon this also: "Now no chastening for the present seemeth to be joyous, but grievous: nevertheless, afterward it yieldeth the peaceable fruit of righteousness" (Hebrews 12:11).

III. THE COMFORT OF GOD IS CLAIMED BY PRAYER (v. 11).

A. Paul had faced "the sentence of death" (v. 9), but the prayers of the saints had "helped" him. So conscious was he of this dependency that in practically all of his letters he made requests for prayer (Romans 15:30, 31; Ephesians 6:18, 19; 1 Thessalonians 5:25; 2 Thessalonians 3:1, 2; 1 Timothy 2:8).

B. Amid life's trials we cannot "trust in ourselves" (v. 9), but must lean upon Him who is able to "raiseth the dead" (v. 9b). Our comfort and consolation *is* in the knowledge that "God is able" (9:8; Ephesians 3:20).

CONCLUSION

The comfort and consolation of God is vouchsafed to us by his Holy Spirit, whom Jesus called "the Comforter" (John 16:7). That which Jesus promised was realized by the struggling church (Acts 9:31), and is available to us.

Isaiah 40:1, 2 is the prologue to the second part of his prophecy—a message of divine comfort and consolation. Here God addresses the prophet, his spokesman, to proclaim comfort to Israel, for her trial of captivity is to be terminated by the grace of God. (This text served as the inspiration for Handel's great oratorio, "The Messiah.") Likewise, everyone captured and enslaved by sin can know release and comfort through Jesus Christ, the Messiah. Matthew 3:1-3 is our authority for applying this prophecy to the coming of the divine Redeemer.

ILLUSTRATION

Sensitivity. A wit once remarked, "Whose cruel idea was it for the word 'lisp' to have an 's' in it?" When we think about it, that word choice does seem insensitive, at the least! In all seriousness though, if we have experienced a disability, tragedy, or heartbreak, we should become more sensitive to those who likewise suffer. The fruit of our personal struggle is experience to understand the pain of another.

The Role of Conscience

2 Corinthians 1:12-14

What is "conscience"? *Random House Dictionary* defines it as "the complex of ethical or moral principles that controls or inhibits the actions or thoughts of an individual." Conscience is not a teacher or leader, but a monitor or censor. It monitors, or censors, or criticizes according to what it has been taught. It can do no better than its knowledge or understanding. It has been characterized as "a moral scrutinizer," or "an organ of moral judgment" (Funk & Wagnalls). Should we "let our conscience be our guide"? Not if our conscience is an ignoramus!

The word "conscience" is not used in the Old Testament, and in ordinary Greek usage it had a vague meaning. In the New Testament it has the distinct meaning of living in integrity—living up to one's understanding of right and wrong. Morality is simply a disposition to live up to one's understanding of what is true and right. The immoral person is one guilty of self-perjury—denying or abusing what one knows to be right. This presupposes instruction. An educated conscience honored is a "good conscience."

In this passage of Scripture, we see that the conscience plays three roles in the life of the Christian.

I. ITS ROLE IN RELATION TO SELF

A. Living in conformity to a well-informed conscience gives one a strong confidence.

1. "Our rejoicing"; rather, "our boast" (v. 12) is not in a prideful or haughty spirit, but in simplicity (holiness) and sincerity after the will of God, not according to fleshly wisdom.
2. Paul's rejoicing or boasting is in agreement with his conscience or moral conviction that he has been sincere and honest in all his dealings with the Corinthians and the Word.

B. A person can withstand the slings and arrows of outrageous fortune and the censure of both friends and foes, if he can sincerely feel that he has been true to himself and to his trust (1 Peter 3:16).

C. A person's moral strength rests in his honest self-approval and his ability "not to think of himself more highly than he ought to think; but to think soberly" (Romans 12:3). A man is weak only when his conscience upholds his accuser.

II. ITS ROLE IN SOCIAL RELATIONSHIPS

A. People are social beings. In the very beginning God determined that "It is not good that the man should be alone" (Genesis 2:18). The fulfilled life is determined by meaningful and happy human relationships.

B. This being true, it is little wonder that God's revelation places such strong emphasis upon fellowship. Fellowship means the quality or condition of being a fellow or companion. But such a condition is dependent upon integrity of character. One must live with a good conscience toward others.

C. This is the call and the challenge of Christianity. Christ came to make peace in a fragmented society. Just as *worship* connotes an intimate and reverent communion with the *worthy*, so *fellowship* connotes a close and intimate relationship with our *fellows*. This calls for a pure and sincere conscience. Peter describes our Lord as one in whom "no sin, neither was guile found in his mouth," and urges that we "follow his steps" (1 Peter 2:21, 22). It is said of the multitude of the redeemed that "in their mouth was found no guile" (Revelation 14:5). Our Christian fellowship here on earth should be a foretaste of that which we shall know in Heaven.

III. ITS ROLE IN RELATION TO GOD

A. Can anyone legitimately "boast" in God with all our foibles and failures? Is there any occasion for self-approval?

1. Yes. God wants us to have a sense of security in Him. The psalmist was aware of this: "My soul shall make her boast in the Lord" (34:2); "In God we boast all the day long, and praise thy name for ever" (44:8).
2. God spoke through Jeremiah: "Let him who boasts boast about this: that he understands and knows me" (9:24, NIV). This passage was quoted twice by the apostle Paul—1 Corinthians 1:31 and 2 Corinthians 10:17.

B. To be whole, sound, and moral are the highest of human qualities. David exposed his integrity to examination: "Judge me, O Lord, for I have walked in mine integrity" (Psalm 26:1); "Judge me, O Lord; . . . according to mine integrity" (Psalm 7:8). Only a clear conscience before God could issue such an invitation.

C. The height of one's spiritual well-being is reached when he or she feels accepted and secure in God's presence (Acts 24:16). This sense of well-being is the blessing of a conscience that is clear in relation to God.

ILLUSTRATION

The threefold conscience. Joseph provides a good example of a well-informed conscience. When Potiphar's wife propositioned him he had three responses: (1) How can I perjure my own moral self? (2) How can I commit this offense against my master? (3) How can I do this great sin against God? (See Genesis 39:7-10.)

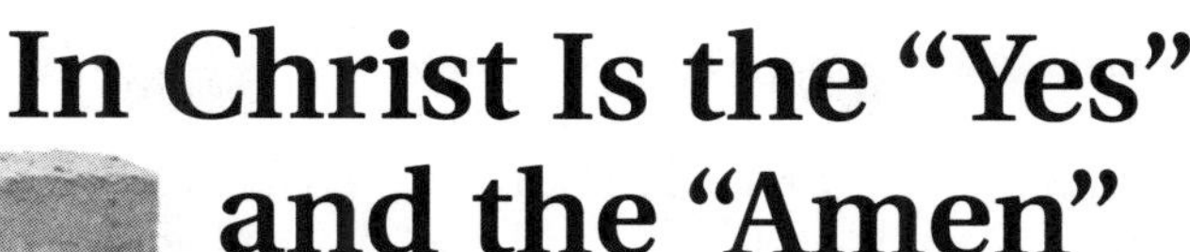

In Christ Is the "Yes" and the "Amen"

2 Corinthians 1:18-22

Charged with being a vacillating "yes" and "no" person, Paul defended himself with a challenging declaration: "For all the promises of God in him are yea, and in him Amen" (v. 20). Why this sudden shift of emphasis? The Corinthians were saying, in effect, "If we cannot depend on Paul's word concerning such a simple matter as his plans to visit us, how do we know that what he preached to us is true?" So he made this strong affirmation. Paul avowed that "All the promises of God" are affirmed, or are fulfilled in Christ—He is the divine "Yes;" and we, by faith, echo his authentication with our own "Amen."

I. GOD HAS MADE PROMISES TO HIS PEOPLE.

A. The "all" indicates the variety of those promises.

1. There are literally hundreds of prophecies dealing with practically every aspect of human life, both physical and spiritual.
2. Many predict historical events such as the captivity of Israel, the overthrow of Babylon, the destruction of Jerusalem, and the return from captivity.
3. The most amazing of these prophecies predict literally hundreds of details about the coming, the life, and the ministry of the Messiah.

B. His promises are trustworthy.

1. God's promises were recognized and honored by Abraham (Romans 4:20, 21).
2. God's promises were declared by Solomon, the wise king: "There hath not failed one word of all his good promise" (1 Kings 8:56).
3. God's promises were fully realized in Christ (Matthew 5:18; Luke 24:44).

II. CHRIST IS THE FULFILLMENT OF ALL GOD'S PROMISES.

A. In Christ, who was preached among them by Paul, there was no ambivalence, but a positive "Yes." In Him all the promises of God came to fruition. (See Acts 3:18.)

B. "In him *was*" (v. 19b). The word *gegenen,* translated "was" in the AV and "has been" in the NIV, literally means "has become." It denotes an accomplished fact.

C. When Jesus cried from the cross "It is finished" (John 19:30), He must have been referring to the whole remedial system which God had been prophesying and perfecting through all the ages.

D. Paul states emphatically: "Jesus Christ was a minister . . . to confirm the promises made unto the fathers" (Romans 15:8).

III. WE GLORIFY GOD BY AFFIRMING THESE TRUTHS.

A. The phrase "unto the glory of God by us" (v. 20) is better translated "by him is also the Amen to God, uttered by us to his glory." In Christ is the "Yes" of ultimate fulfillment of God's promises, and the church utters the "Amen" of faith and grateful praise to God.

B. In this passage, as well as in 1 Corinthians 14:16, we have evidence of the ancient custom of the "Amen." The congregation acknowledged and agreed with the glorious blessings bestowed upon us by the fulfillment of all His "exceeding great and precious promises" (2 Peter 1:4).

1. This praise by the "Amen" is also an expression of our unity in Christ—"with one mind and one mouth" we glorify God (Romans 15:6).
2. We glorify God, not only in our profession, but in all of life (1 Corinthians 6:19, 20; 2 Thessalonians 1:12).

C. Since the "Yes" is in Christ, it is by Him that we have the ability to properly utter the "Amen" to the glory of God (v. 20).

D. God, through Christ, qualifies us for this grace:

1. He "stablisheth us" (v. 21a).
2. He "hath anointed us" (v. 21b).
3. He "hath also sealed us" (v. 22a).
4. He has given us "the earnest of the Spirit" (v. 22b).

E. The "Yea" and the "Amen" are so closely related that in Revelation 1:7 they are treated as identical. Our "Amen" is of the same character as Christ's "Yes"—they both confirm and glorify God. (Note: the *nai amen* is usually translated "Even so, Amen," but the Living Bible gives it as "Yes! Amen!")

CONCLUSION

The church militant is a foretaste of the church triumphant. John witnessed the host of Heaven singing, "To him who sits on the throne and to the Lamb, be praise and honor and glory and power, for ever and ever" (Revelation 5:13, NIV). And the four Living Creatures sanctioned with "Amen" (Revelation 5:14). In Revelation 19:4 the four living creatures are joined by the twenty-four elders, who fell down and worshiped God, saying, "Amen; Alleluia."

ILLUSTRATION

Christ's fulfilling role. Henry P. Liddon of Oxford states, "There are three hundred and thirty-two distinct prophecies in the Old Testament which have been literally fulfilled in Christ." A mathematician has calculated the probability of this occurring to one man as one in 84 followed by 97 zeros!

The Obligation of Forgiveness

2 Corinthians 2:3-11

Several Greek words in the New Testament are translated as "remit," "release," "dismiss," or "forgive." But the word employed by Paul in this text *(charizomai)* means to bestow favor unconditionally—without reservation. It is used of the act of forgiveness whether divine (Ephesians 4:32; Colossians 2:13; 3:13), or human (Luke 7:42; 2 Corinthians 2:7, 10; 12:13; Ephesians 4:32).

Ephesians 4:32 emphasizes the close relationship between the two: human forgiveness is to be patterned after that of the divine. Jesus taught this in His model prayer—"Forgive us our debts, as we forgive our debtors;" and by His affirmation that if we forgive—God will forgive us.(See Matthew 6:12, 14, 15.)

If the prerequisite conditions are met, there is no limitation to Christ's law of forgiveness (Matthew 18:21, 22). Those conditions are repentance and confession (Matthew 18:15-17; Luke 17:3, 4; James 5:16; 1 John 1:9).

The case in view here calls for a strict application of the divine principle of forgiveness because it has to do with a very serious transgression.

I. THE OCCASION FOR FORGIVENESS

A. There was a grievous problem in the Corinthian church—a brother, nebulously referred to as "any," "a man," (vv. 5, 6), "anyone," (NIV, v. 5), "the man," (LB, v. 5), and as "him," (vv. 7, 8), had suffered a moral lapse to the embarrassment and injury of the church. Possibly, this could be the same case that Paul wrote about in 1 Corinthians 5—so scandalous that it is "not so much as named among the Gentiles" (v. 1).

B. This lapse was so grievous to Paul that he had wept over it (v. 4) and he had written a letter concerning it (vv. 3, 4, 9).

C. Apparently, the church had taken his letter to heart and had dealt with the matter to Paul's satisfaction (v. 6), for he concurs in their judgment and forgiveness (v. 10).

II. THE NECESSITY FOR FORGIVENESS

A. It is a Christian obligation. "Ye ought rather to forgive . . ." (v. 7). This involves Christian morality—morality is the disposition to do what is known to be right. God is ultimately moral because he always does what is best.

B. We must mirror God's character—"even as God for Christ's sake hath forgiven you" (Ephesians 4:32). If we claim to be children of God we must reflect the character of God.

C. Christ's example "constraineth" (compels, motivates) us (5:14). He has left us an example that "ye should follow his steps" (1 Peter 2:21).

D. We forgive for the restoration and salvation of the sinner (v. 7b). The primary purpose of church discipline is the redemption of the offender (1 Corinthians 5:5).

E. We are under the scrutiny of Christ, our Master (v. 10), and we must face up to the question, "What would Jesus do?"

F. When we forgive, we thwart the stratagems of the devil (v. 11).

III. THE QUALITY OF FORGIVENESS

A. It must be a confirmation of Christian love (v. 8). "Confirm your love"—i.e., *ratify* your love—make sure the offender knows that he or she is fully forgiven and restored.

B. It must be without limit—"As far as the east is from the west" (Psalm 103:12); "Though your sins be as scarlet . . . "(Isaiah 1:18).

C. Its aim must be benevolent: "For edification, and not for your destruction" (10:8; 13:10).

ILLUSTRATIONS

Forgiveness when slandered. Greek military leader, Pittacus, was severely criticized by the poet and satirist, Alcaeus. Yet when he had arrested Alcaeus he released him, saying, "Forgiveness is better than revenge."

Superior to punishment. The philosopher Epictetus wrote: "Forgiveness is better than punishment; for the one is proof of a gentle, the other of a savage nature."

An invitation. A church bulletin contained this misprint: "The choir invites any member of the congregation who enjoys *sinning* to join the choir." It would be great if all of our church bulletins could accurately read: "This congregation invites anyone weary of sinning to seek forgiveness here."

The Triumph of the Gospel

2 Corinthians 2:14–3:6

As a Roman citizen, the apostle Paul must have been acquainted with a "Triumph." This name was given to a great pageant of celebration for a military victory. The victorious generals, dressed in silken robes, mounted on highly decorated horses; the army in dress, marching in cadence, with polished weapons of war; slaves bearing great masses of booty; prisoners in chains and bound for the sacrifice—all marched through the streets of the city to the deafening shouts and tumultuous roar of the amassed multitudes. It was a moving sight. (Flavius Josephus, first-century Jewish historian, gives a detailed description of a Roman triumphal procession in *Wars of the Jews, Book VII,* Chapter V, sections 4 and 5.)

Paul dares to employ the term "triumphal procession" to describe the victories of the gospel: "God . . . always leads us in triumphal procession in Christ" (v. 14, NIV). Is this claim too ambitious? Apparently not. Paul had a glowing sense of victory, and a great appreciation for what God was doing in the world through the gospel. In the light of history, this exalted claim was justified.

I. PAUL'S PERSONAL EXPERIENCE WITH THE GOSPEL

A. As Saul of Tarsus, a loyal Pharisee, and strong opponent of Christianity, he had lost his battle against the church (Acts 8:1; 9:1-30). His opposition had been wholehearted and unrelenting. He could later say:

1. "I persecuted this way unto the death, binding and delivering into prisons both men and women" (Acts 22:4). He was an ardent defender of the most deep-seated convictions and prejudices of Judaism, and thought that he was doing the will of God (Acts 26:9).
2. "Many of the saints did I shut up in prison . . . when they were put to death, I gave my voice against them. And I punished them oft in every synagogue, and compelled them to blaspheme; and being exceedingly mad against them, I persecuted them even unto strange cities" (26:10, 11).

B. But after his encounter with Christ on the Damascus road, he had been recommissioned by a new and greater authority:

1. To Ananias the Lord said of Saul, "He is a chosen vessel unto me, to bear my name before the Gentiles, and kings, and the children of Israel" (Acts 9:15).
2. To Saul God said: "I have appeared unto thee for this purpose, to make thee a minister and a witness" (26:16).

C. Paul had experienced the triumph of the gospel so that he could say, "I am crucified with Christ: . . . and the life which I now live in the flesh I live by the faith of the Son of God, who loved me, and gave himself for me" (Galatians 2:20).

II. THE WIDER TRIUMPH OF THE GOSPEL

A. In addition to his own personal encounter with Christ and the gospel, Paul had witnessed, or knew about, the amazing triumph of Christianity:

1. Triumph was obvious in Jerusalem: 3,000 converts at Pentecost (Acts 2:41); daily additions (2:47); "about five thousand" (4:4); "multitudes both of men and women" (5:14); the number multiplied (9:31).
2. Triumph was obvious in widening circles: Judea, Samaria, Phoenicia, probably Africa (8:26), and all the regions to which all the Pentecostal witnesses had returned (2:9-11).

B. At the time of this writing (middle of the third missionary journey), Paul had personally carried the gospel to Syria, Cilicia, Pisidia, Galatia, Macedonia, Achaia, and possibly to Illyricum and other regions (Romans 15:19).

C. He could later write that the gospel, of which he was a minister, "was preached to every creature which is under heaven" (Colossians 1:23). All in one brief lifetime! During these travels and ministries he had turned multitudes "from darkness to light" (Acts 26:18). A *triumph* indeed!

CONCLUSION

In light of all this, Paul's response was, "Thanks be unto God"(v. 14). He also rejoiced that believers are always led to "triumph in Christ."

ILLUSTRATIONS

Sweet savor. A loving husband may enjoy the scent of his wife's perfume that lingers on him well after he leaves her presence. Paul alluded to the incense that hung in the air in a Roman triumphal procession. Just as a husband is reminded by fragrance of the one who has captured his heart, and the Romans, by fragrance, were reminded of the conquering empire, the world experiences the victorious church by the "sweet savor" of the truly redeemed.

Tell them it's over! On January 8, 1815, General Andrew Jackson commanded an American force that defeated an attacking British regiment in the Battle of New Orleans. More than 2,000 men lost their lives in this bloody clash, but the strife was unnecessary. The War of 1812 had ended fifteen days earlier. Tragically, the news of the signing of the peace treaty had not yet reached the battlefield.

The war against Satan is over, his defeat complete by the work of Jesus. Yet many die in unnecessary battles because the news of this victory has yet to reach them.

The Gospel's Greater Glory

2 Corinthians 3:9-16

A large section of this epistle (2:14–6:10) deals with the nature and function of ministry: the victorious progress of the gospel (2:14–3:6), the superiority of the gospel over the Law (3:7–4:6), the heavenly treasure in earthen vessels (4:7-18), the earthly versus the heavenly home (5:1-10), and the ministry of reconciliation (5:11–6:10).

In this passage, Paul argues the gospel's greater glory in comparison with the Law. He introduces the subject by a series of questions: If the ministry that entailed death came with glory, how much greater glory is accorded that which brings life? If the ministry that condemns is glorious, how much more glorious is that which brings righteousness? If that which is fading away came with glory, how much greater is the glory of that which does not fade away?

I. PAUL'S FORCEFUL AFFIRMATION

A. "What was glorious [the Law] has no glory now in comparison with the surpassing glory [of the gospel]" (3:10, NIV).

B. The Law, "written and engraven in stones," was glorious (3:7).

1. It was glorious because it was a revelation from God and expressed His will for mankind.
2. This glory was symbolized by the divine manifestations which accompanied its pronouncement (Exodus 19:14-24; 20:18) and by the glow on the face of its administrator, Moses (Exodus 34:30).
3. But that glory has faded in the light of a greater revelation (vv. 9-11). The transfiguration of Jesus clearly depicted His superiority over the Law and the prophets (Matthew 17:1-8).

II. PAUL'S ARGUMENT

A. The Law was only a temporary measure, "which glory was to be done away."

B. The Law had been prophesied and was understood.

1. God had announced its abrogation centuries before through the prophet Jeremiah (Jeremiah 31:31; Hebrews 8:10).
2. Jesus had symbolized a "new testament" in the establishing of the Lord's Supper (Matthew 26:28).
3. Paul understood that the Law was merely a "schoolmaster" to prepare for

something better (Galatians 3:24, 25).

C. There are reasons the Law failed.

1. It was a "ministry that brought death" (AV); a "ministry that condemns" (NIV). It brings death and condemns because man's failure (inability) to keep it was penalized by death (Exodus 22:20; 35:2; Leviticus 20:2, 10-12).
2. The Law was weak in that it placed the burden upon unrighteous man who is unable, but grace is strong because the burden is borne by God who is righteous and able.
3. Under the Law man was required to prove his righteousness, but under grace man enjoys an imputed righteousness—a "ministration of righteousness" (v. 9; Romans 4:5, 6). A greater glory, indeed!

III. PAUL'S AUTHORIZATION FOR THIS DECLARATION

A. "Our sufficiency is of God; who also hath made us able ministers of the new testament" (vv. 5b, 6a).

B. Paul's claim to such ordination was not prideful boasting. He was always self-abnegating. In 1 Corinthians 15:9 he states that he was the least of the apostles, and not worthy to be called one. To the Ephesians he declared that he was "the least of all saints" (Ephesians 3:8).

C. But now he speaks with boldness and "plainness of speech" (v. 12), because "[God] hath made us able ministers" (v. 6). Writing to Timothy, he thanks Christ that He "enabled me . . . putting me into the ministry" (1 Timothy 1:12).

D. His apology: "Seeing then, that we have such hope, we use great plainness of speech" (v. 12)—"we are very bold" (NIV). He does not shrink from declaring the message, but he feels no call to embellish it with the flowery speech so common with the public orators of his day (1 Corinthians 2:1).

CONCLUSION

All who cling to the Law are veiled, as was the face of Moses, but for those who turn to the Lord the veil is taken away (v. 16). "Now the Lord is that Spirit: and where the Spirit of the Lord is, there is liberty" (v. 17). Jesus taught,"If the Son therefore shall make you free, ye shall be free indeed" (John 8:36).

ILLUSTRATION

Moses' radiance. When Michelangelo made his famous sculpture of Moses, he put horns on him. His acquaintance with the Bible was the Latin version, which translated Exodus 34:29, 30 as "beams" or "horns," and being a dutiful son of the Medieval Church, he felt that he had to put horns on Moses. However, he had such ambivalence about the horns that he practically obscured them with locks of curly hair!

A Glorious Transformation

2 Corinthians 3:18

There is a common saying to the effect that "You can't make a silk purse out of a sow's ear," but that is precisely what God is attempting to do with us. Generally speaking, there are only two themes or messages in the New Testament. First, a message of justification, addressed to the sinner; second, a message of sanctification, addressed to the saint. Our text is from the latter category, and it tells us three things about attaining the glorious transformation: the procedure, the effect, and the agency.

I. THE PROCEDURE FOR OBTAINING THE GLORIOUS TRANSFORMATION

A. "With unveiled [open] face beholding as in a glass the glory of the Lord." There are two steps here: negative and positive.

B. The negative: the covered (or veiled) face. We must strip off all attitudes that prevent our seeing the truth and glory of God as revealed in Christ.

1. What are those face-veils? They are many and varied: preconceptions, prejudices, biases, unbelief, enmity toward God, etc.
2. Out of the unregenerate heart comes evil thoughts, murders, adulteries, fornications, thefts, false witness, railings, coveting, wickedness, deceit, lasciviousness, lust, pride, foolishness (Matthew l5:19; Mark 7:21, 22).
3. The prophet Isaiah spoke of such as "the covering cast over all people, and the veil that is spread over all nations" (Isaiah 25:7).

C. The positive: "beholding as in a glass the glory of the Lord."

1. To "behold" calls for careful scrutiny. Jesus often employed the word to center attention.
2. No study of books, no exposition of doctrines, no observance of rituals, can do for us so much as the daily "looking unto Jesus the author and finisher of our faith" (Hebrews 12:2).

II. THE EFFECT OF THIS PROCEDURE

A. "[We] are changed into the same image from glory to glory"—step by step, degree by degree, from one stage to another.

B. This mutation of character is a process of growth—we grow as we understand

and apply. It involves a conscious effort to understand and meet the ideal. It demands a strict morality—the disposition and desire to do what we ought.

C. As we comprehend truth and right, and conform our lives to them, they become a part of the very fabric of our character and effect the transformation of which we are speaking.

D. Though this growth is slow, it is not to be an excuse for puny effort and low living. Petrified wood was once altogether vegetable, but is now altogether mineral. But the change required a lot of time and patience!

III. THE AGENCY OR MEANS OF THIS TRANSFORMATION

A. "By the Spirit of the Lord."

B. This statement is variously translated. But however it is translated, Paul is obviously identifying the Spirit with the Lord. In verse 17 he says, "Now the Lord is that Spirit: and where the Spirit of the Lord is, there is liberty."

C. In our carnal nature we are the sons of Adam, but in our transformed spiritual nature we are the sons of God. "For the law of the Spirit of life in Christ Jesus hath made me free from the law of sin and death" (Romans 8:2).

D. Because He is the Spirit, the Lord has access to the inmost recesses of our being where He hallows, renews, and glorifies the personality in which He dwells and to whom He makes himself graciously and divinely known. Apparently, there is no limit to this transforming process.

ILLUSTRATIONS

Spiritual alchemy. During the Middle Ages many were enamored with the concept of alchemy. Alchemy was a fabled process that could change the base into the precious—lead to gold, stones to diamonds, etc. But that dream faded. The only true alchemy is spiritual, and God is the Great Alchemist! "If any man be in Christ, he is a new creature"! (2 Corinthians 5:17).

A serious look. A serious look at the Christ can cause a major transformation. Lew Wallace served as a major general in the Union army during the Civil War. Urged by his dear friend Robert Ingersoll, the famous skeptic, he agreed to write a book that would forever destroy the "myth" of Christianity. The credibility of such a famous military figure would certainly bring many to accept his conclusions.

For two years, Mr. Wallace studied in the leading libraries of Europe and America, seeking information which would enable him to write such a book. While writing the second chapter of this work he suddenly found himself on his knees, crying out, "My Lord, and my God." The One he had determined to expose as a fraud had captured him, and he became a Christian. Later, Lew Wallace wrote *Ben Hur*, probably the greatest novel that has ever been written concerning the time of Christ.

We Have This Ministry

2 Corinthians 4:1; 5:18-20

In 2 Corinthians 2:14–6:10, Paul discusses the nature of the Christian ministry. He discusses the triumph of the gospel (2:14–3:6), the superiority of the gospel over the Law (3:7–4:6), heavenly treasure in earthen vessels (4:7-18), the contrast between the earthly and the heavenly abode (5:1-10), and the gospel as a means to reconciliation (5:11–6:10). Finally, Paul gives the key to his vigorous labor: "For the love of Christ constraineth us" (5:14). Moral compulsion issues from a deep sense of indebtedness and gratitude. The psalmist asked: "What shall I render unto the LORD for all his benefits toward me?" (Psalm 116:12). Paul answers: "We have a ministry to perform."

I. THE NATURE OF THIS MINISTRY

A. It is a service. The word he used is *diakonian* which means "servant," "attendant," or "minister." (From it we get our word "deacon.") This "ministry" is to be like that of Christ (Matthew 20:28; Luke 22:27; John 13:4, 5; Philippians 2:7).

B. It is a ministry of reconciliation, of making peace between man and God. This peace is the result of justification, and justification is the reward of faith (Romans 5:1).

C. Therefore, this ministry entails preaching that which produces faith, for "faith cometh by hearing, and hearing by the word of God" (Romans 10:17). The source of that content is "the new testament" (2 Corinthians 3:6).

D. Though this ministry seems humanly impossible, with God nothing is impossible (Mark 10:27). "[He] hath made us able ministers" (2 Corinthians 3:6).

II. THE TWOFOLD BURDEN OF THIS MINISTRY

A. We preach the remission of sins through faith in Jesus Christ.

1. In His farewell message, Jesus said that "repentance and remission of sins should be preached in his name among all nations" (Luke 24:47).
2. The first gospel sermon carried the message, "Repent, and be baptized . . . for the remission of sins" (Acts 2:38).
3. Paul declares that Jesus Christ is the One "in whom we have redemption

through his blood, even the forgiveness of sins" (Colossians 1:14).

4. Paul was firm in his conviction that the gospel of Christ "is the power of God unto salvation to every one that believeth" (Romans 1:16).

B. We preach reconciliation with God through Jesus.

1. Though God was the offended, He provided a means of reconciliation with rebellious and disobedient man (Ephesians 2:18; Colossians 1:20).
2. This reconciliation makes for peace among men (Luke 2:14; Ephesians 2:14-17). Peace is God's intent for mankind. "In every nation . . . The word which God sent . . . preaching peace by Jesus Christ" (Acts 10:35, 36). Paul's admonition is to "follow after the things which make for peace, and things wherewith one may edify another" (Romans 14:19).

III. THE DIGNITY OF THIS MINISTRY

A. Ministers of the gospel are "ambassadors for Christ" (2 Corinthians 5:20). They are the honored representatives of the King of kings, and speak for Him who has "all power . . . in heaven and in earth" (Matthew 28:18).

B. The message he carries is not from the messenger, but from the portfolio entrusted to him. Paul asserted, "We preach not ourselves, but Christ Jesus the Lord; and ourselves your servants for Jesus' sake" (2 Corinthians 4:5).

C. It has been aptly said: "The ministry is the function of *imperfect* men presenting the *perfect* Man to *perfectible* men."

D. All who accept the grace of God and conform to His will are accounted as "perfect" (Colossians 1:28; 4:12; 1 Thessalonians 3:10; 2 Timothy 3:17), and the preacher of the gospel has the honor of bringing men to faith and obedience.

CONCLUSION

The preacher of the Word occupies an enviable position. Paul states it succinctly: "We are laborers together with God" (1 Corinthians 3:9). What an honor to be God's coworkers, God's partners!

ILLUSTRATION

Dignity of the ministry. During the minister's illness, a church bulletin contained this blooper: "GOD IS GOOD! The preacher is better."

It is indeed an honor to serve in the ministry, but it is not because of the minister's virtue! We are granted this honorable task through the grace of our Lord.

Christ, the Image of God

2 Corinthians 4:4

Our English word "image" is from the Latin *imago,* meaning a copy, an imitation, a representation. From it we get the word "imitate." An image is intended to faithfully picture the reality which it represents.

Apparently, Paul favored this term as a description of Christ. In our text he speaks of Christ as "the image of God." In Colossians 1:15 he calls him "the image of the invisible God." This is not extravagant language, for the very being and perfection of God are revealed in the person of Christ. Let us note some of the respects in which Christ reflects God.

I. HIS ETERNAL EXISTENCE IS AFFIRMED THROUGHOUT THE BIBLE.

A. Isaiah describes the coming Christ as "The Everlasting Father" (9:6).

B. Micah speaks of "[His] goings forth have been of old, from everlasting" (5:2).

C. "In the beginning was the Word . . . with God . . . was God" (John 1:1).

D. Paul wrote, "He is before all things" (Colossians 1:17).

E. Jesus himself said He was with God "before the world was" (John 17:5).
1. God loved Him "before the foundation of the world" (John 17:24).
2. "I am Alpha and Omega, the beginning and the end, the first and the last" (Revelation 22:13).

F. The writer of Hebrews describes Him as "having neither beginning of days, nor end of life" (7:3).

II. HIS DIVINITY IS THE KEYSTONE OF THE CHRISTIAN FAITH.

A. God himself testified, "This is my beloved Son" (Matthew 3:17; 17:5).

B. Christ testified on behalf of himself.
1. "I and my Father are one" (John 10:30).
2. "He that seeth me seeth him that sent me" (John 12:45).
3. "If ye had known me, ye should have known my Father also" (John 14:7).
4. "He that hath seen me hath seen the Father" (John 14:9).

C. The apostles witnessed to Christ's divinity.

1. Peter: "Thou art the Christ, the Son of the living God" (Matthew 16:16).
2. John: "The Word [Christ] was with God, and the Word was God" (John 1:1).
3. Paul: "God was manifest in the flesh" (1 Timothy 3:16).

III. HIS CREATIVE POWER WAS THE AGENT OF GOD IN ALL CREATION.

A. "All things were made by him" (John 1:3).

B. "All things were created by him" (Colossians 1:16).

C. "By whom [Christ] also he [God] made the worlds" (Hebrews 1:2).

D. He creates man anew (2 Corinthians 5:17). "My Father worketh hitherto, and I work" (John 5:17).

IV. HIS MASTERY OF THE UNIVERSE MAKES HIM LORD OF ALL.

A. Christ claimed this mastery. "All power is given unto me" (Matthew 28:18).

B. Christ demonstrated this mastery. (See, for example, Matthew 8:23-27; 9:18-26.)

C. John the Baptist testified of this mastery (John 3:35).

D. The apostle Paul echoes this same testimony (1 Corinthians 15:24; Ephesians 1:22).

V. THE FULLNESS THAT DWELLS IN HIM IS BY THE PLEASURE OF GOD.

A. His fullness (sufficiency) is the source of all our blessing (John 1:16).

B. "It pleased the Father that in him should all fulness dwell" (Colossians 1:19).

C. "In him dwelleth all the fulness of the Godhead bodily" (Colossians 2:9). "To us there is but one God, the Father, of whom are all things, and we in him; and one Lord Jesus Christ, by whom are all things, and we by him" (1 Corinthians 8:6).

ILLUSTRATION

The incomparable Christ. He is the Bread of Life, the thirst-quenching Water, the Rock of security, the Good Shepherd, the eternal Sacrifice, the Deliverer, the Ransomer, the Pearl of great price, the Lily of the Valley, our Passover, our Friend, the Living Way, the Resurrection and the Life, the Savior, the Messiah, the Door, the Way, the Truth, the Life, the Redeemer, the Forgiver, the Lover, the Holy One, the Perfect One, the Sinless One, the Understanding One, the Wisdom of God, the Presence of God, the Great Physician—the list of accolades found in Scripture to describe Jesus is almost endless. THE IMAGE OF GOD, INDEED!

Treasure in Earthen Vessels

2 Corinthians 4:7

The term "treasure" is prominent in the Scriptures. As a noun it connotes any thing or person greatly valued or highly prized, something of uncommon worth or significance. In its verbal form it indicates the act of bestowing great esteem or showing high honor or respect. In our text it is used as a noun.

The unique significance of this "treasure" is that it is a gift of God, which gives it a rank or value far above any earthly treasures. Most of the things treasured here on earth pale into insignificance by comparison to the endowments of God.

I. THE TRUST—"THIS TREASURE"

A. The "treasure" being considered is the message of salvation by grace through Jesus Christ (2 Corinthians 4:6; Romans 3:24; Titus 2:11).

B. This message is couched in the "glorious gospel" which is to be preached (2 Corinthians 4:4; John 6:63; Romans 1:16).

C. Christ, the central figure in this gospel, is a gift from God (John 3:16; 4:10; 2 Corinthians 9:15), and He reveals God to us (John 1:18; 10:30; 14:10).

D. In Christ are "all the treasures of wisdom and knowledge" (Colossians 2:2, 3); so Paul could say, "I determined not to know any thing among you, save Jesus Christ, and him crucified" (1 Corinthians 2:2).

E. In view of this great trust the apostle cried, "O, the depth of the riches both of the wisdom and knowledge of God! how unsearchable are his judgments, and his ways past finding out!" (Romans 11:33).

F. This is the treasure of which Paul speaks. It is "the power of God unto salvation" (Romans 1:16).

II. THE TRUSTEES—"EARTHEN VESSELS"

A. These "earthen vessels" ("jars of clay" [NIV]; "pots of earthenware" [NEV]; "a perishable container" [LB]) are human agents, people who are "the ministers of Christ, and stewards of the mysteries of God" (1 Corinthians 4:1).

B. Agents are tools, instruments, and means to an end, not the end in themselves. They are used by an outside power for accomplishing a set purpose. As Paul said, "We preach not ourselves, but Christ Jesus the Lord" (2 Corinthians 4:5).

C. Tools, agencies, and means are weak and dispensable. "The excellency of the power may be of God, and not of us" (v. 7). Then he proceeds to speak of his own weakness. He is troubled, perplexed, persecuted, and always dying (2 Corinthians 4:8-11; 12:10; Philippians 3:8). It has been well said that "God buries His workmen, but He carries on His work."

D. Even though these "earthen vessels" are weak and transitory, they have a "high calling" (Philippians 3:14). They are honored with being "ambassadors" of the eternal King (2 Corinthians 5:20; Ephesians 6:20). As such they bear witness to the "unsearchable riches of Christ" (Ephesians 3:8).

E. Like earthly ambassadors, these messengers carry a portfolio with the authorization of the King. Jesus affirms, "The Father which sent me, he gave me a commandment, what I should say, and what I should speak" (John 12:49).

CONCLUSION

"I determined not to know any thing among you, save Jesus Christ, and him crucified. And my speech and my preaching was not with enticing words of man's wisdom, but in demonstration of the Spirit and of power" (1 Corinthians 2:2, 4).

"Though I preach the gospel, I have nothing to glory of: for necessity is laid upon me; yea, woe is unto me, if I preach not the gospel!" (1 Corinthians 9:16).

"We preach not ourselves, but Christ Jesus the Lord; and ourselves your servants for Jesus' sake" (2 Corinthians 4:5).

ILLUSTRATION

Contaminated treasure. A recent study showed that 42 percent of all paper money carries some sort of infectious disease. The treasure that many long for can literally kill them! Contrast that to the treasure that we carry as believers. We offer the treasure of God, salvation through grace, a treasure that gives life rather than threatens it.

Four Cardinal Doctrines

2 Corinthians 4:13-15

The apostle Paul had the genius to put a whole doctrinal sermon in one sentence. Here he takes his text from Psalm 116:10, and with one dip of his pen he writes a fourfold declaration of faith. He embraces the faith of his fathers: "As it is written, I believed, . . . we also believe, and therefore speak" (v. 13). This faith is grounded in knowledge—"knowing." Faith may be defined as a moving conviction resulting from an intellectual evaluation of credible evidence. The four parts of this faith-statement are all fundamental to the Christian system, and are fully treated throughout the New Testament Scripture.

I. GOD RAISED JESUS FROM THE DEAD (v. 14).

A. This is the cornerstone of the Christian edifice.

1. Paul gives the definitive argument on this point in 1 Corinthians 15:14-17.
2. His resurrection was predicted by Jesus himself (Matthew 16:21; 26:32; Mark 9:9; 14:28; John 2:19).
3. The doctrine of the resurrection was preached by the apostles (Acts 2:23, 24; 3:14, 15; 4:33; 10:39-41; 17:2, 3).
4. Resurrection from the dead was a major theme of the New Testament writers (Romans 1:4; 4:25; 10:9; 1 Corinthians 15:4; Ephesians 1:20; 1 Thessalonians 4:14; 2 Timothy 2:8; 1 Peter 1:3).

B. The resurrection of Jesus was attested by many witnesses (Acts 13:30, 31; 1 Corinthians 15:4-8). He made numerous postresurrection appearances, more than a dozen of them recorded. He was seen in His resurrected body by more than 500 witnesses.

C. His resurrection was authenticated by unquestioned proofs (Acts 1:3). The AV translates this as "infallible proofs," the RSV, "many proofs," the NIV, "convincing proofs," the NEB, "ample proofs," the LB, "proved in many ways."

II. WE ALSO SHALL BE RAISED FROM THE DEAD (v. 14).

A. This is the solemn promise of the Lord Jesus Christ (John 5:25, 28, 29; 6:40; 11:25).

B. This promise was reiterated by the Holy Spirit through the preaching of the gospel (Acts 24:15; 1 Corinthians 15:22, 23; 2 Corinthians 4:14).

C. Resurrection from the dead is the most profound hope of the Christian (Acts 24:15; Colossians 1:5; Titus 2:13).

D. This hope rests upon the fact of the resurrection of Jesus Christ (1 Peter 1:3).

III. ALL THINGS ARE DESIGNED FOR OUR GOOD (v. 15).

A. The classic text for this proposition is Romans 8:28. The AV says, "All *things* work together for good." The NIV says,"In all things God works for the good." The agent for "good" is not *things*, but God.

B. God's goodness is designed for our redemption (Romans 2:4). It is not the will of God "that any should perish, but that all should come to repentance" (2 Peter 3:9).

C. This work for good is a matter of grace, not of merit (Acts 15:11; Romans 3:24; 5:15; 11:6; Ephesians 2:5; Titus 2:11; 3:7).

IV. THANKSGIVING FOR THIS GRACE OVERFLOWS TO THE GLORY OF GOD (v. 15).

A. We glorify God by our word.

1. "With one mind and one mouth [we] glorify God" (Romans 15:6).
2. "Giving thanks always for all things unto God and the Father in the name of our Lord Jesus Christ" (Ephesians 5:20; 1 Thessalonians 5:18; Hebrews 13:15).
3. "Speak as the oracles of God . . . that God in all things may be glorified" (1 Peter 4:11).
4. "Giving thanks unto the Father, who hath made us fit to be partakers [through Christ] of the inheritance of the saints" (Colossians 1:12).
5. "Let the peace of God rule in your hearts . . . and be ye thankful" (Colossians 3:15).

B. We glorify God by our lives.

1. Our consecration brings glory (Romans 12:1; 1 Corinthians 6:20).
2. Our good works bring glory (Matthew 5:16; 1 Timothy 6:18; Titus 2:7; Hebrews 10:24; James 2:17, 18; 1 Peter 2:12).
3. Our fruit-bearing brings glory (John 15:8, 16; Romans 7:4; Philippians 1:11, 4:17; Colossians 1:10).

CONCLUSION

Our hope rests upon the immutability of God, who cannot lie (Hebrews 6:17-19). Furthermore, this hope is an anchor that holds us steady amid the raging storms. Finally, this "lively hope" is given substance by the resurrection of Christ (1 Peter 1:3).

ILLUSTRATION

Glorifying God in our lives. In Ephesians 2:8-10, Paul summarizes the Christian life in three prepositional phrases: "By grace, through faith, unto good works."

Our Ultimate Victory

2 Corinthians 5:1-8

The glorious hope posited in the New Testament is that of eternal life, the exchange of this mortal for an immortal existence. Herein is an amazing advance from the Old Testament where the concept is almost totally absent. It contains only a few obscure hints (2 Samuel 12:23; Job 19:26; Psalm 49:15; 71:20; Daniel 12:2; Hosea 13:14). In fact, the terms "immortality" and "eternal life" are not found in the Old Testament Scriptures. This is not surprising when we note that it was Jesus Christ who "brought life and immortality to light through the gospel" (2 Timothy 1:10).

In contrast, those concepts loom large in the New Testament, especially in the preaching and writings of the apostle Paul. In this passage, Paul gives us three powerful pictures of our eternal hope.

I. THE GREAT CONTRAST—THE BUILDING OF GOD IS SUPERIOR TO THE EARTHLY HOUSE (v. 1).

A. The great contrast is indicated immediately by two vastly differing terms: "tabernacle" (tent), and "building"—one temporary, the other permanent.

B. The superiority of the latter is suggested by four descriptive terms. It is of God. It is not of human device. It is eternal. It is in a heavenly setting. In John 14:2, Jesus described it as a heavenly complex of many mansions (abodes).

C. This earthly dwelling is subject to groans (vv. 2, 4), "burdens" (v. 4), troubles, distress, perplexity, and persecutions (4:8, 9). The heavenly is eagerly desired "that mortality might be swallowed up of life" (v. 4).

D. The heavenly home knows none of these earthly woes (Revelation 21:4), and its character is almost beyond our ability to comprehend (vv. 10-23).

II. THE GREAT DESIGNER AND BUILDER—GOD MADE US FOR THIS VERY PURPOSE (v. 5).

A. The translations of this verse vary, but in any case the emphasis is upon God as the prime actor. Whether He designed us for the blessing, or the blessing for us, is of little consequence. He is the operating force in the whole scheme.

B. God is able to "save them to the uttermost" (Hebrews 7:25) because:

1. He is the creator of all (Acts 14:15; 17:24; Hebrews 11:3). As such, "He knoweth our frame" (Psalm 103:14).
2. He is the Redeemer (Luke 1:68; Ephesians 4:30; 2 Timothy 4:18; 2 Peter 2:9). He performs this redeeming work through Jesus Christ (Romans 3:24; 1 Corinthians 1:30; Galatians 3:13; Colossians 1:14; Titus 2:14; Hebrews 9:12).
3. He is the sustainer (Deuteronomy 33:27; Psalm 31:23; Isaiah 40:10; Acts 17:28).
4. Most of all, the New Testament reveals Him as a loving Father (Matthew 6:9; John 16:27; 2 Corinthians 6:18; 2 Peter 3:9).

III. THE GREAT CONFIDENCE—DEATH IN CHRIST LEADS TO ETERNAL LIFE (vv. 5-8).

A. Paul is strong in this affirmation. "We know" (v. 1); "We are always confident" (vv. 6, 8). To Timothy he could write, "I know whom I have believed, and am persuaded that he is able to keep that which I have committed unto him against that day" (2 Timothy 1:12).

B. This confidence is based upon the reality of the resurrection of Jesus Christ from the dead.

1. The fact of the resurrection is the foundation stone of the Christian faith, as Paul states in 1 Corinthians 15:1-8, 14.
2. The resurrection was the central theme of the gospel as it was preached by the apostles (Acts 2:23, 24; 3:14, 15; 4:33; 10:39-41; 17:2, 3).

C. Trusting in the validity of this claim, Paul reasoned, "I count all things but loss for . . . my Lord . . . that I may know him, and the power of his resurrection, if by any means I might attain unto the resurrection of the dead" (Philippians 3:8-11).

CONCLUSION

This heavenly home is an unmerited blessing, an unearned inheritance (Acts 20:32; 26:18; Colossians 1:12; 3:24; Titus 3:5-7; 1 Peter 1:4). It is the gift of God, an expression of the "riches of his grace"(Ephesians 1:7; 2:7; Philippians 4:19). Yet we can claim it by faith in and obedience to God's missionary to earth, Jesus Christ (Matthew 7:21; Romans 16:25-27). "But thanks be to God, who always leads us in triumphal procession in Christ" (2 Corinthians 2:14, NIV).

ILLUSTRATION

Confidence despite persecution. Pastor Mehdi Dibaj of Iran had converted from Islam to Christianity. He stood accused of translating Christian radio programs and books into the Farsi language. When placed on trial for his life, he testified, "Of all the prophets, Jesus alone was resurrected from the dead, and He remains our living mediator forever. I gave my life into His hands." Though spared execution because of international pressure, he was found dead in a park shortly after his trial in 1994, presumably a victim of an Islamic death squad.

Wherefore We Labor

2 Corinthians 5:9

The apostle has just been reflecting upon the glorious prospect of exchanging this earthly tabernacle for the "building of God, . . . eternal in the heavens" (5:1). He might have remained in that state of transport, but his sense of duty calls him back to the present. He does not allow contemplation of the heavenly to blind him to the labor assigned him in this earthly state. He is constrained by the love of Christ (5:14) to follow His example: "I must work the works of him that sent me" (John 9:4). Let's examine this labor together.

I. THE NATURE OF THIS LABOR IS TO PREACH AND TEACH (MATTHEW 28:19, 20).

A. Preaching is presenting the evidences for Jesus' messiahship and persuading alien sinners to accept Him as Savior and Lord.

1. To this end Jesus instructed His disciples (Luke 24:47, 48).
2. His witnesses were faithful to this mission (Acts 5:42; 10:42).
3. Though this message was "foolishness" to many, it "pleased God" to save the world by it (1 Corinthians 1:21, 23; Romans 1:16).
4. As "least of the apostles" Paul could say, "I labored more abundantly than they all" (1 Corinthians 15:9, 10).
5. The "constraint" of Christ's love (5:14) was such that Paul felt, "Woe is unto me, if I preach not the gospel!" (1 Corinthians 9:16).

B. Teaching is the naturalization of new citizens.

1. "Let the word of Christ dwell in you richly" for the purpose of "teaching and admonishing" (Colossians 3:16).
2. Paul's instructions to Timothy: "These things command and teach" (1 Timothy 4:11; 6:2); "commit thou to faithful men, who shall be able to teach others also" (2 Timothy 2:2).
3. The purpose of teaching: to develop maturity (Ephesians 4:13; 2 Timothy 3:17).

II. THE OBJECTIVE OF THIS LABOR IS TWOFOLD.

A. We seek to satisfy and glorify God.

1. Our text states Paul's motivation: that "we may be accepted of him." This is a common sentiment in the New Testament. Jesus worked in such a way that God was "well pleased" (Matthew 3:17; 17:5). Paul encouraged the churches

saying, "We beseech you, brethren, and exhort you by the Lord Jesus, . . . how ye ought to walk and to please God" (1 Thessalonians 4:1). John agreed. "We do those things that are pleasing in his sight" (1 John 3:22).

2. Not only are we to please God, but also to glorify Him in our labor. Jesus encouraged His disciples to "let your light so shine before men, that they may see your good works, and glorify your Father which is in heaven" (Matthew 5:16). "Herein is my Father glorified, that ye bear much fruit" (John 15:8). Paul told the church at Rome to live in such a way "that ye may with one mind and one mouth glorify God, even the Father of our Lord Jesus Christ" (Romans 15:6). Likewise, Peter wrote that we are to "speak as the oracles of God . . . that God in all things may be glorified" (1 Peter 4:11).

B. We seek the redemption and salvation of humankind.

1. Redemption is our purchase price (Romans 3:24; 1 Corinthians 6:20; 7:23; Galatians 3:13; Colossians 1:14; Titus 2:14; 1 Peter 1:18, 19).
2. Salvation is also the conservation and development of our potential (Ephesians 4:22-24; Titus 2:11, 12; James 1:21; 1 Peter 2:11, 12; 2 Peter 1:4-10).

III. THE REWARDS OF THIS LABOR ARE TEMPORAL AND ETERNAL.

A. Our labor is rewarded in this world.

1. "Seek ye first . . . and all these things shall be added unto you" (Matthew 6:33).
2. "[You] shall not receive manifold more in this present time" (Luke 18:30).
3. We will receive a new and more abundant life (John 10:10; Romans 6:4; 2 Corinthians 5:17; Ephesians 4:24).
4. We will seek new horizons, having a fuller vision (Ephesians 3:17-19).

B. Our labor is rewarded in the world to come. Those rewards include:

1. A new body (1 Corinthians 15:53).
2. A new home (John 14:2, 3; 2 Corinthians 5:1).
3. A new fellowship (1 Corinthians 1:9; 2 John 9).
4. A crown of righteousness (2 Timothy 4:8).
5. A crown of glory (1 Peter 5:4).

CONCLUSION

Work, for the night is coming, Work through the morning hours;
Work while the dew is sparkling, Work 'mid springing flowers;
Work when the day grows brighter, Work in the glowing sun;
Work, for the night is coming, When man's work is done. —Annie L. Walker

ILLUSTRATION

Rewards of labor. Although many may consider work as merely a means to earn income, it is obvious that in this country millions work for other reasons. Statistics show that 48.8 percent of all Americans participate in some regular volunteer service. We seek rewards for labor beyond the material.

The Motivating Power of Love

2 Corinthians 5:14

The character of a person's life can be changed by a change of motivation. This truth is dramatically illustrated in the life of Saul of Tarsus, who became the apostle Paul. His new motivation was "the love of Christ."

I. THE CHARACTER OF CHRIST'S LOVE

A. The love of Jesus was first demonstrated in His becoming human.

1. Though on an equality with God, He did not consider this rank as something to be held onto, but He "made himself nothing" (Philippians 2:7, NIV).
2. His submission to the will of God was complete. "I came down from heaven, not to do mine own will, but the will of him that sent me" (John 6:38).

B. The very fact that Jesus would assume a human nature is a condescension of such magnitude as to be almost beyond human conception.

1. In His identification with sinful mankind He was subjected to all of our trials and temptations (Hebrews 4:15).
2. Truly, "though he was rich, yet for your [our] sakes he became poor, that ye through his poverty might be rich" (2 Corinthians 8:9).
3. William R. Newell expressed this love in his hymn, "At Calvary." "O the love that drew salvation's plan!/O the grace that brought it down to man!"

C. Jesus manifested His love in His life among humankind.

1. He came not to be ministered to, but to minister (Matthew 20:28). "The Son of Man is come to seek and to save that which was lost" (Luke 19:10). "God sent not his Son into the world to condemn the world; but that the world through him might be saved" (John 3:17). "I am come that they might have life, and that they might have it more abundantly" (John 10:10).
2. The apostle Paul had it right. "Christ Jesus came into the world to save sinners" (1 Timothy 1:15).

D. Jesus' love is evidenced in the manner of His death.

1. This was a transcendent proof of His love. "Greater love hath no man than this, that a man lay down his life for his friends" (John 15:13).
2. This supreme sacrifice was voluntary. He said, "No man taketh it [my life] from me, but I lay it down of myself" (John 10:18). This fact is confirmed repeatedly by the apostle Paul (Galatians 1:4; Ephesians 5:2; Titus 2:14).

E. Jesus shows His love by His continuous intercession for us.

1. "It is Christ that died . . . who also maketh intercession for us" (Romans 8:34).
2. "He is able also to save them to the uttermost . . . seeing he ever liveth to make intercession for them" (Hebrews 7:25).

II. THE EFFECT OF THIS LOVE UPON THE APOSTLE

A. Paul declared, "For the love of Christ constraineth us" (5:14). "Constraineth" indicates a progression—its influence is continuous. It was not some passing fancy or emotion. Its motivating power became more compelling as the love of Christ was increasingly appreciated.

B. It "constrained" him—compelled, obliged him—to live for and to serve the Christ. He expressed this commitment clearly: "The life which I now live in the flesh I live by the faith of the Son of God, who loved me, and gave himself for me" (Galatians 2:20).

C. The love of Christ overmastered him: he was no longer his own, because he had been "bought with a price" (1 Corinthians 6:20).

D. This endeavor entails:

1. Living a blameless life, free of moral culpability.
2. Seeking to show forth Christ in character, spirit, conduct, and holy ambition.
3. Submitting to the will of Christ in all our earthly endeavors by asking the question: "What would Jesus do?"
4. Seeking to extend the kingdom of Christ on earth for His glory, fulfilling the prayer: "Thy kingdom come, Thy will be done" (Matthew 6:10).
5. Loving one another even as He loves us.

CONCLUSION

The love of Christ sets a new pattern of life before us, and we should strive to "follow his steps" (1 Peter 2:21). This new motive provides us with an inner spiritual power to pursue the goal that is set before us (Hebrews 12:1).

ILLUSTRATIONS

The reason for His love. Paul wrote "For he hath made him, who knew no sin, to be sin for us, that we might be made the righteousness of God in him" (2 Corinthians 5:21). St. Augustine paraphrased this verse saying, "In Christ God became such as we are in order that in Christ we might become such as He is."

Seeing God. A preschool girl was diligently composing a picture. When her teacher asked about her artwork, the tot replied, "I'm drawing God." Smiling, the teacher corrected her, "But no one knows what God looks like." With innocent enthusiasm the girl replied, "They will in a minute."

Though God cannot be pictured with pencil and crayon, His likeness can be seen in the life of our loving Savior.

The Christian: A New Creation

2 Corinthians 5:17

The apostle's firm affirmation is that "if any man be in Christ, he is a new creature [creation]." This is a totally revolutionary concept, incomprehensible apart from an act of God. It is comparable to the problem which Nicodemus had in comprehending the new birth (John 3:4).

The proposition is introduced with a "Therefore"—a reflexive word which alludes to something prior. That "something" is the fact that if Christ "died for all, then were all dead" (5:14). In another place, Paul affirms that we were "dead in trespasses and sins" (Ephesians 2:1). Being dead, man's only hope of life again is through a new creation, living "unto him which died for them, and rose again" (5:15). He avows that if we are in Christ we are indeed new creatures.

I. HOW THIS NEWNESS IS ACCOMPLISHED

A The transformation takes place by the power and the grace of God. Just as God was the originating cause in the first creation, so is He in the second. Just as Christ was the instrumental cause in the first creation, so is He in the second.

B. The transformation takes place by the believer's death with Christ. This is argued eloquently in Romans 6:3-6. When we are baptized into Christ, we die to sin and become a new person in Him. (See also Galatians 3:27.)

C. The transformation takes place by becoming participants in the life of Christ. "If ye then be risen with Christ, seek those things which are above" (Colossians 3:1). We become "partakers of the divine nature, having escaped the corruption that is in the world" (2 Peter 1:4).

II. HOW THIS NEWNESS MANIFESTS ITSELF

A. The newness manifests itself in the believer's spirit, speech, behavior, purposes, desires, and total character. This is commonly called being "born again."

B. Our text affirms, "all things are become new." The "all" is inclusive. There is no part of the believer's life that is exempt from this new orientation.

C. While not yet completed, the glorious transformation has begun. "Old things are passed away." The new motive is operating, and the new life is developing.

III. HOW THIS NEWNESS OF LIFE EVIDENCES OUR CHRISTIANITY

A. Have we more than a mere profession? How do we prove it to the world about us? James gives us the measure of "pure religion and undefiled" (1:27). Then he adds: "I will show thee my faith by my works" (2:18).

B. This standard applies to all people, for all who are in Christ are new creatures. There is to be a decided change in the best people as well as in the worst.

C. This newness must be a present reality, not something to be realized in some far-off and distant place. By becoming new creatures in Christ, and living in Him here and now, we become fit subjects for the new world which He has promised.

CONCLUSION

"Behold, I make all things new" (Revelation 21:5). The new creation, projected for the consummation of the age, is to be the abode of those who are now experiencing the new creation of humanity. The comforting words of Jesus were: "I go to prepare a place for you" (John 14:2). In the "new Jerusalem" (Revelation 21:2), there will be room for all who have been created anew in Christ Jesus.

ILLUSTRATIONS

An amazing transformation. The "new man" is comparable to a grain of popped corn: it is the same grain, but it has gone through an amazing transformation. What the heat does for the corn, the grace of God does for us.

A new man. Cyprian, a wealthy pagan, was converted to Christ and eventually became Bishop of Carthage. Upon conversion he forsook his opulent lifestyle, gave his goods and money to the poor, and took a vow of chastity. His testimony was: "A second birth created me a new man by means of the Spirit breathed from heaven." He died a martyr under the Emperor Valerian in A.D. 258 at the age of 58.

The Ministry of Reconciliation

2 Corinthians 5:18, 19

"Reconciliation" is a word that encapsulates the whole purpose of the Christian gospel—the restoration of a fallen world to the favor and fellowship of God. The "ministry of reconciliation" involves three parties: God, Christ, and the proclaimer of the Good News. God designed the plan, Christ is His agent, and people are His ministers.

I. GOD IS THE DESIGNING CAUSE.

A. From the time humankind disrupted its relationship with God by rebellion and disobedience, God has been effecting a scheme of redemption.

1. The first announcement of a messianic Redeemer is that the "seed" of the woman shall eventually bruise the head of evil (Genesis 3:15).
2. This projected "seed" was promised to Abraham (Genesis 12:3; 17), and Paul identified Abraham's seed with Christ (Galatians 3:16).
3. The saviorhood of God was recognized and celebrated by many Old Testament worthies (Psalm 37:39; Isaiah 12:2; 25:9; Jeremiah 23:3; Zephaniah 3:17).

B. This plan of reconciliation came to complete fruition with the advent, ministry, atoning death, resurrection, and exaltation of Christ.

1. Zacharias, father of John the Baptist, announced by the Holy Spirit: "God . . . hath visited and redeemed his people, and hath raised up a horn of salvation for us" (Luke 1:68, 69).
2. Paul declared, "The grace of God that bringeth salvation hath appeared to all men," and that "God . . . will have all men to be saved" (Titus 2:11; 1 Timothy 2:3, 4).
3. Peter noted that "The Lord is not slack concerning his promise, . . . but is long-suffering toward us, not willing that any should perish" (2 Peter 3:9).

II. CHRIST IS THE INSTRUMENTAL CAUSE.

A. Christ is the agent through whom God works.

1. He was the instrumental cause in the original creation (John 1:3, 10; Colossians 1:16; Hebrews 1:2; 2:10).
2. He is God's agent in redemption and reconciliation (2 Corinthians 5:18).
3. As the guiding principle of His life, He quoted Psalm 40:8, "Lo, I come to do thy will, O God" (Hebrews 10:7, 9).

4. He confirmed this intent in His life and ministry (Matthew 21:42; John 6:38; 8:29).

B. He faithfully fulfilled His mission.

1. His life conformed to the prophetic picture drawn by Isaiah (Isaiah 53:5). His one consuming desire was to do His Father's will, "I do always those things that please him" (John 8:29). (See John 17:4; 19:30.)
2. The completion and adequacy of His redemptive work was understood and proclaimed by His disciples: Paul (1 Corinthians 15:3; 2 Corinthians 5:15); Peter (1 Peter 2:21-24; 3:18); and the Hebrew writer (Hebrews 2:17; 13:12).

III. THE MINISTER IS THE PROCLAIMER.

A. The minister's mandate is to "preach the word" (2 Timothy 4:2).

B. The minister must recognize the "scandal" (a literal translation of the Greek) of the gospel (1 Corinthians 1:21).

C. The minister must be faithful to the message (Acts 5:42; 2 Timothy 4:5).

D. The minister must not be contentious, but gentle (2 Timothy 2:24-26).

E. The minister must have a sense of necessity and urgency (1 Corinthians 9:16).

CONCLUSION

Karl Barth, the great Swiss theologian, described preaching as "the impossible, but indispensable task." The world-changing challenge of the gospel ministry is, "Be ye reconciled to God" (2 Corinthians 5:20).

ILLUSTRATION

The burden of the ministry. A church newsletter was said to report, "The concert held in Fellowship Hall was a great success. Special thanks are due to the minister's daughter, who labored the whole evening at the piano, which as usual fell upon her."

God has designed the plan of salvation, Christ implemented the plan, but the burden of proclaiming the plan falls upon believers, ministers of reconciliation.

Ambassadors for Christ

2 Corinthians 5:20

"Now we are ambassadors for Christ" (AV); "We are therefore Christ's ambassadors" (NIV). The "now" or the "therefore" reflect upon a prior consideration—namely, the reconciling gospel of Christ. An ambassador holds an honored position. He or she is a personally chosen emissary of the head of one state to that of another, and he or she carries all the delegated authority essential to the execution of the mission. Such is the political usage of the term. However, it is also used in social, economic, and religious contexts. The latter applies to our text from the apostle Paul. Apparently, the apostle liked the term to represent his ministry, for here he asserts that "We are ambassadors for Christ," and in Ephesians 6:20, writing from prison, he describes himself as "an ambassador in bonds."

I. THE AMBASSADOR'S QUALIFICATIONS

A. At first ambassadors were chosen on the basis of friendship or close political affiliation, but experience (sometimes embarrassing) soon demonstrated the importance of merit as a primary consideration.

B. A primary qualification for a Christian ambassador is spiritual maturity.

1. New Testament practice supports this view (Luke 6:13-16; John 20:21; 2 Timothy 2:2).
2. The Greek word *(presbeus)* here translated "ambassador" is also translated "elder" when referring to church leaders (Acts 14:23; 1 Timothy 5:17; Titus 1:5). When Paul refers to himself in Philemon 9 as "the aged" he uses the same word, and it is translated as "ambassador" in the NEB.
3. In such usage of the term "elder" the emphasis is not upon chronological age, but upon maturity, sagacity, and understanding. Paul describes such a person as "sober, grave, temperate, sound in faith, in charity, in patience" (Titus 2:2).

C. Furthermore, the Christian ambassador must have strong convictions concerning the character and mission of Jesus Christ.

1. The Christian ambassador proclaims that Jesus is God's Son (Matthew 16:16; John 1:1, 2; Romans 1:4; 9:5; Colossians 2:9; 1 Timothy 3:16; Hebrews 1:3).
2. The Christian ambassador proclaims that Jesus is the promised Messiah (Matthew 11:3ff; 26:63, 64; Luke 2:11, 26; 4:41; John 1:41; 4:25, 26; 6:69; 11:27; Acts 9:22; 17:3; 1 John 5:1).

3. The Christian ambassador proclaims that in Jesus alone is salvation (John 3:16; Acts 4:12; 1 Corinthians 2:2; 3:11).

II. THE AMBASSADOR'S EQUIPMENT

A. Every ambassador carries a portfolio—an elaborate leather case or large envelope containing credentials and instructions. It provides authorization for carrying out negotiations on behalf of his or her country, and defending its political, economic, and cultural interests.

B. Likewise, the Christian ambassador has his portfolio—the Bible, the Word of God. It contains his directions and responsibilities.

C. All who aspire to this honored function go forth under the divine marching orders of the Great Commission (Matthew 28:19, 20). It is sufficient for every occasion and need (2 Timothy 3:16, 17; Hebrews 4:12).

III. THE AMBASSADOR'S MISSION

A. The ambassador must represent Christ to the world (Galatians 2:20). We dare not preach ourselves and our opinions (2 Corinthians 4:5).

B. The ambassador must be an example "in word, in conversation, in charity, in spirit, in faith, in purity" (1 Timothy 4:12).

C. The ambassador must preach the Word in season and out of season. We must reprove, rebuke, exhort with all patience and teaching (2 Timothy 4:2).

D. The ambassador must preach Christ crucified for the sins of mankind, "the power of God, and the wisdom of God" (1 Corinthians 1:23, 24).

CONCLUSION

If a political ambassador represents his or her country and uses every possible means to promote her interests, how much more should those who represent God to a sinful world be diligent!

ILLUSTRATIONS

History of ambassadors. The ancient Greeks were the first to exchange diplomatic representatives with other nations, but in 1815 (the year of Waterloo) the Congress of Vienna set up an international system of exchange. In 1893 the United States sent her first representatives to France, Germany, Great Britain, and Italy.

The mission of the ambassador. Often the main mast of an old sailing vessel would be broken off and carried away by a violent storm. The crew would have to rig up what was called a "jury-mast"—a temporary substitute until the mast could be replaced.

Christ is the real head of the church, but we as Christians are now "in Christ's stead" (2 Corinthians 5:20), doing His work till He returns.

Paul's Beseeching Plea

2 Corinthians 6:1-13

"Beseech" (AV), "entreat" (RSV), "urge" (NIV), "beg" (LB), and "appeal" (NEB) are all words of serious and strong persuasion. So, however the Greek word *parakaloumen* is translated, it is evident that Paul was writing from great concern. That concern was that his preaching of the grace of God might not have been in vain, that is, without its effect being shown in the lives of his converts. Therefore, his "beseeching" is that they not sully the gospel by low living. He is conscious of the fact that the "vain" lives of his converts may be used to discredit his ministry of the gospel among them. To this he responds by describing the nature of his ministry.

I. THE NATURE OF HIS MINISTRY AMONG THE CORINTHIANS

A. Uncharacteristically, and no doubt unwillingly, he "approves" or "commends" himself—something which he is always loath to do. In the eleventh chapter he calls this foolishness into which he has been pressed by his opposition (v. 17).

1. He affirms that he has striven to give no offense or grounds upon which they could disparage his ministry (v. 3).
2. He proceeds to demonstrate that his ministry has not been directed by selfish motives, but has been a total outpouring of himself on their behalf—"in all things [in every way] approving [commending] ourselves as the ministers of God" (v. 4).

B. Paul calls to their attention the evidence of his selfless ministry: "in great endurance; in troubles, hardships, and distresses; in beatings, imprisonments and riots; in hard work, sleepless nights and hunger; in purity, understanding, patience and kindness; in the Holy Spirit and in sincere love; in truthful speech and in the power of God; with weapons of righteousness on the right hand and left; through glory and dishonor, bad report and good report; genuine, yet regarded as impostors; known, yet regarded as unknown; dying, and yet we live on; beaten, and yet not killed; sorrowful, yet always rejoicing; poor, yet making many rich; having nothing, and yet possessing everything" (vv. 4-10, NIV).

C. In all this, his character and disposition have been attested by the spiritual quality of his life (v. 6), by the truth and force of his message (v. 7), and by his reaction to the accusations and sufferings inflicted upon him (vv. 9, 10). This is his vindication and the way he "commends" himself to their judgment.

II. WHAT DOES THE APOSTLE ASK OF THE CORINTHIANS?

A. He commands in verse 13: "Now for a recompense in the same, . . . be ye also enlarged"; "As a fair exchange . . . open wide your hearts also" (NIV).

1. He appeals to their sense of justice: Give to me as I am giving to you. As always, he assures them of his steadfast love before he offers any criticism.
2. He points out that they are denying themselves. "Ye are not straitened in us, but ye are straitened in your own bowels." The NIV makes this statement more meaningful saying, "We are not withholding our affection from you, but you are withholding yours from us" (6:12).

B. This is a matter of the heart

1. "Bowels" is a Jewish term for the seat of affections (Philippians 1:8; 2:1; Colossians 3:12; Philemon 20). The meaning is expressed today by the term "heart."
2. The scriptural "heart" is the whole conscious person—intellect, emotion, and volition (will). So a person is a triune being, just as God is triune. Our love of God and others must involve our whole self.

C. This call to enlargement is an invitation to an expansion of being which Jesus came to offer—the "more abundant life" (John 10:10).

D. Furthermore, Paul declares that such an enlargement of thinking, feeling, and willing will enable us to "comprehend with all saints what is the breadth, and length, and depth, and height . . . [that] which passeth knowledge" (Ephesians 3:18, 19).

E. Such is the transformation to which we are called in Christ!

CONCLUSION

The third Commandment of the Decalogue is not primarily directed against cursing or swearing, but against the false and empty use of the name of God. To call ourselves children of God without demonstrating it in life is to "take the name of the LORD thy God in vain" (Exodus 20:7).

ILLUSTRATION

Walking our talk. The problem of making life match profession is as old as the church itself. The oldest Christian sermon on record, outside of the New Testament, is by the *Shepherd of Hermas* (second century): "For the Gentiles when they hear from our mouth the oracles of God, marvel at them for their beauty and greatness; then, when they discover that our works are not worthy of the words which we speak, forthwith they betake themselves to blasphemy, saying that it is an idle story and a delusion."

A Call to Separation

2 Corinthians 6:14–7:1

Some scholars think that this section may be all or part of Paul's *first* letter to the Corinthians (1 Corinthians 5:9). If true, then what we know as 1 Corinthians is actually second; and if (as some hold) 2 Corinthians 10:1–13:10 is the severe letter mentioned in 2 Corinthians 7 and 9, then our second letter would be the fourth! Some justification for the former judgment is that 7:2 returns to the subject of 6:13—Paul's appeal for personal acceptance. He is very anxious to heal any wounds occasioned by his former letter (third Corinthians) and to reconcile any estrangement caused thereby. The problem addressed in this section (or letter) is that of the separation of Christians from the entanglements of the world. It was a problem of long standing in the Corinthian church, and Paul deals with it in at least three of his letters (1 Corinthians 5:9, 11; 2 Corinthians 5:7, 8, 11-13; 6:14-17; 11:8-10, 21). That this was a grievous matter with the apostle is evident, not only in his Corinthian correspondence, but in all his writings (Ephesians 5:7, 11, 15; 2 Thessalonians 3:6).

I. PAUL'S FIRM ADMONITION (v. 14)

A. Do not be unequally yoked!

1. The primary thrust concerns intermarriage with unbelievers, but this is only a part of the problem of separation from worldly dispositions and behavior. He proceeds immediately to widen the range of his exhortation.
2. This is a matter of grave concern because marriage is the ultimate means of sharing one's life with another. A faulty marriage can blast one's life as well as his relationship with God.

B. Separation from the world was a vital issue with Paul.

1. To the Ephesians he gave strong counsel: "Be not ye therefore partakers with them. . . . have no fellowship with the unfruitful works of darkness . . . walk circumspectly" (Ephesians 5:7, 11, 15).
2. To the Thessalonians he was even bolder: ""We command you, yourselves . . . withdraw from every brother that walketh disorderly. . . . If any man obey not our word . . . have no company with him" (2 Thessalonians 3:6, 14).

II. PAUL'S SOCRATIC ARGUMENT (vv. 14b-16a)

A. Socrates formalized the method of teaching by questioning. But God had employed this method centuries before Socrates appeared on the scene (Job 38; Isaiah 40:12-28).

B. Paul's employment of this method consisted of these questions (vv. 14-16):
1. "What fellowship hath righteousness with unrighteousness?"
2. "What communion hath light with darkness?"
3. "What concord hath Christ with Belial [Satan]?"
4. "What part hath he that believeth with an infidel?"
5. "What agreement hath the temple of God with idols?"

C. To the rational mind the answer to all these questions is a resounding, "None!" The Corinthians could not have failed to get it!

III. THE BASIS FOR THIS DRASTIC CALL (v. 16b)

A. "Ye are the temple of God." The apostle emphasizes this fact frequently (1 Corinthians 3:16; 6:19).
1. Since "the temple of God is holy" there is compelling reason for separation from worldly entanglements.
2. As the temple was made holy by purification and dedication, so is the church.

B. He supports this amazing declaration by quoting God's Word through Zechariah: "they shall be my people, and I will be their God" (8:8).

C. Paul saw the fulfillment of this promise in the church (Ephesians 2:19-22).

IV. THE REWARD FOR THIS SEPARATION (vv. 17, 18)

A. The condition: "Wherefore come out from among them, and be ye separate" (v. 17). It has been pointed out that all of God's promises are conditional. This indicates the synergistic nature of soteriology, that salvation is completed when we respond to the grace of God.

B. The threefold promise:
1. God says, "I will receive you" (v. 17). This acceptance is attained through Jesus Christ (Romans 5:15; Ephesians 1:6).
2. "[I] will be a Father unto you" (v. 18). What an amazing promise! (Romans 8:15-17).
3. "Ye shall be my sons and daughters" (v. 18). We are the objects of a loving adoption (John 1:12; Galatians 4:5, 6).

C. The inescapable conclusion: "Having therefore these promises, dearly beloved, let us cleanse ourselves . . . perfecting holiness in the fear of God" (7:1).

ILLUSTRATION

Separation. Anthony, an unwitting founder of monasticism, was born to great wealth in Egypt about A.D. 200. Upon conversion to Christ he took seriously the admonition: "If thou wilt be perfect, go and sell that thou hast, and give to the poor" (Matthew 19:21). He gave his lands to the poor villagers, sold his other holdings, and gave the money to the poor.

Repentance: A Cause for Rejoicing

2 Corinthians 7:8-11

Repentance is the first condition of forgiveness and salvation. The sinner is at enmity with God, and cannot have peace with God until he changes his mind and reverses his life pattern.

I. THE GOSPEL'S EMPHASIS UPON REPENTANCE

A. It was the keynote of John the Baptist: "Repent ye: for the kingdom of heaven is at hand" (Matthew 3:2).

B. It was stated bluntly by Jesus during His earthly ministry: "Except ye repent, ye shall all likewise perish" (Luke 13:3, 5).

C. In His commissioning of the disciples Jesus said, "Repentance and remission of sins should be preached in his name among all nations" (Luke 24:47).

D. It was preached by the first gospel heralds:

1. At Pentecost: "Repent, and be baptized . . . for the remission of sins, and ye shall receive the gift of the Holy Ghost" (Acts 2:38).
2. At the temple: "Repent . . . that your sins may be blotted out" (Acts 3:19).
3. To Simon the Sorcerer: "Repent therefore of this thy wickedness, . . . [that] the thought of thine heart may be forgiven thee" (Acts 8:22).
4. Paul to the Athenians: "The times of this ignorance God winked at; but now commandeth all men every where to repent" (Acts 17:30).

II. AN EXAMPLE OF GENUINE REPENTANCE

A. In the case before us, both an individual and the congregation were involved. Even though this is a specific case, it provided a good example which can be applied generally.

B. The test of genuine repentance is the altered conduct. John the Baptist demanded "fruits meet [worthy, in keeping] for repentance" (Matthew 3:8). Paul preached that Jews and Gentiles "should repent and turn to God, and do works meet for repentance" (Acts 26:20).

C. What evidences of genuine repentance did the Corinthian church show? (v. 11).

1. Paul urges: "See what this godly sorrow has produced in you" (NIV). Then

he lists at least seven worthy elements: "what carefulness" (earnest consideration); "what clearing of yourselves" (apology, self-defense); "what indignation" (against themselves for neglect of duty); "what fear" (of their injury to the church); "what vehement desire" (to see Paul and make amends); "what zeal" (to make things right and to do the right thing); and "what revenge" (eagerness to see justice done).

2. The apostle's satisfaction with their response to this problem and his letter is indicated in his response: "In all things [at every point] ye have approved [proved] yourselves to be clear [innocent] in this matter."
3. He says in effect, "Despite your previous tolerance of impropriety, your action upon receiving my letter has vindicated your character."

III. SUCH REPENTANCE IS CAUSE FOR REJOICING.

A. Addressing this immediate situation, Paul says, "Now I rejoice . . . that ye sorrowed to repentance" (v. 9).

B. On a wider scope, Jesus declared, "Joy shall be in heaven over one sinner that repenteth" (Luke 15:7).

C. Luke 15 is the great chapter on lostness. Here Jesus narrates three parables to illustrate the disposition of God toward sinners: the lost sheep, the lost coin, the lost son. In every case there is rejoicing upon recovery.

D. The heavenly hosts join in this rejoicing: "There is joy in the presence of the angels of God over one sinner that repenteth" (Luke 15:10).

CONCLUSION

Repentance is a recognition of our destitute condition and a turning to God for forgiveness and salvation. This must be a sincere volitional act—an action of the will.

ILLUSTRATION

Results of repentance. Poet John Milton penned this heartfelt query:
"Miserable me! Which way shall I fly—
Infinite wrath, and infinite despair?
Which way I fly is hell; myself am hell;
And in the lowest deep a lower deep
Still threatening to devour me, opens wide,
To which the hell I suffer seems a heaven.
O then, at last relent! Is there no place
Left for repentance, none for pardon left?!!"

The Bible provides a positive answer to this question. "Let the wicked forsake his way, and the unrighteous man his thoughts: and let him return unto the LORD, and he will have mercy upon him; and to our God, for he will abundantly pardon" (Isaiah 55:7).

From Sorrow to Salvation

2 Corinthians 7:9-11

The context of this passage is Paul's concern for the effect of his letter of reprimand for the Corinthians' laxity toward a breach of Christian ethics; but amid that discourse he pronounces a profound trilogy: Godly sorrow—Repentance—Salvation. These three stages follow in logical and redemptive order and form the outline of the whole soteriological process: we come to an awakening of conscience regarding the enormity of our offense toward God; we make a conscious decision to turn our lives around; and God, in His mercy and grace, grants us salvation through His Son, Jesus Christ.

I. GODLY SORROW

A. The AV phrase "godly sorrow" is not enlarged upon by the RSV or the NIV, but some light is given by verse 9, "made sorry after a godly manner," and verse 11, "ye sorrowed after a godly sort."

B. The NEB speaks of a "wound which is borne in God's way," and the LB speaks of sorrow that God uses to turn us away from sin and toward repentance. So "godly sorrow" is a sorrow that God can use for our redemption.

C. The literal translation of verse 9 *(elupethete yar kata theon)* is: "for we are grieved according to God"; and the same "according to God" is used in verse 11. The literal reading of "godly sorrow" in verse 10 is, "for the according to God grief."

D. In all three of these verses the sense appears to be "according to God," and this is contrasted with "according to the world." The one leads to repentance and salvation, the other leads to death. These verses distinguish between a morbid sorrow which leads to despair and death and the God-ordained grief that leads to repentance and life. Compare, for example, the remorse of Judas and the penitence of Peter.

E. Godly sorrow is to be sorrowful in God's way. It sees sin as God sees it. God hates sin for itself, because of what it is; the world hates or mourns, not over sin, but over its consequences. Godly sorrow leads one to grieve that he or she has sinned; worldly sorrow grieves that sin has brought suffering.

II. REPENTANCE

A. Repentance is the golden door to salvation. The key to it is volition, the human will. Humankind can open it or leave it shut.

B. This is true, in effect, because it is a reversal of man's fall. Just as man fell from the grace of God by a willful act, so man can be restored to God's grace by a willful act. *Metanois* is an active word—it denotes man's move toward God; salvation is God's move toward man.

C. So central and crucial is repentance in the God-man equation that it is prominent in both the Old and New Testaments:

1. It was the message constantly thundered by the prophets to the nation of Israel.
2. It was the message of John the Baptist, last of the prophets and the forerunner of Christ.
3. It was a prominent part of the teaching of Jesus.
4. It was the keynote of the first gospel sermon.
5. It is urged even in the last book of the Bible.

III. SALVATION

A. Salvation is the gift of God.

B. It is mediated through Jesus Christ.

C. It is available to all.

D. It is conditioned upon faith and obedience.

CONCLUSION

The hope of salvation rests upon the integrity of God "that cannot lie" (Titus 1:2; Hebrews 6:18). God was the original, and is the greatest, promise keeper! "He is faithful that promised" (Hebrews 10:23).

ILLUSTRATION

Most important choice. Shakespeare wrote, "There is a tide in the affairs of men—which taken at the flood, leads on to fortune; omitted, all the voyage of their life is bound in shallows and in miseries" (Julius Caesar, Act IV, Scene 3).

This certainly is an apt description of the impact of repentance. When we choose to "surf the wave of repentance," it draws us into the rich depths of God. If we do not, we simply go no deeper in our relationship with our Father.

An Inspirational Example

2 Corinthians 8:1-15

The subject of a "special offering" is of no permanent significance, but the principle involved here is—the duty of helping Christian brethren in need. Apparently, this relief project for the Judean Christians was a general undertaking among all the churches of Paul's acquaintance, and had been under way for over a year (v. 10). Since the Corinthians had been lagging at the task, Paul cites the example of the Macedonian churches as an inspiration to immediate action. "We want you to know" (v. 1, NIV). An ancient proverb says that "comparisons are odious," but sometimes they serve a justifiable end. So Paul wants them to see how "the grace of God" (v. 1) works among those of a "willing mind" (v. 12). Under Roman government all the area north of the isthmus was called "Macedonia," so that Paul's description would have included Philippi, Thessalonica, Berea, and possibly other localities.

I. HOW "THE GRACE OF GOD" WAS MANIFEST AMONG THE MACEDONIANS

A. Despite "a great trial of affliction" and "deep poverty" they responded heartily to this need (v. 2).

1. Their "trial of affliction" had come in the form of persecution which is reflected in 1 Thessalonians 1:6; 2:14 and Acts 16:20; 17:5.
2. Their "deep poverty" stemmed from at least two known sources: the oppression of their Roman conquerors, and the succession of civil wars fought on their soil before Augustus became sole ruler.

B. God's grace enabled them to go beyond human expectations in "the riches of their liberality" (v. 2).

1. Grace had endowed them with two of the loveliest qualities of Christian character: joy and liberality.
2. Consequently, they were able to give "beyond their power" and beyond what Paul had expected of them (vv. 3, 5).

C. Grace enabled them to comprehend the obligations of fellowship in the Christian brotherhood (v. 4; Acts 6:1-6; 11:29; 20:35; Ephesians 4:28).

D. Grace made it incumbent that they first give themselves "to the Lord" (v. 5). It was a matter of love responding to love (1 John 4:19).

II. PAUL'S APPEAL TO THE CORINTHIANS

A. He commends their faith, utterance (speech), knowledge, earnestness, and then urges them to "abound in this grace also" (v. 7).

B. He has no desire to coerce, but only to "prove the sincerity of [their] love" (v. 8).

C. He undergirds his whole appeal by citing the example of Christ: His position in glory and His divine prerogatives were sacrificed for our good; so we, as His disciples, ought to expend ourselves for the good of our fellow people.

D. He cautiously offers a word of advice and encouragement: "Now, do it! Finish the job!"

1. You have talked about it for a year, now get busy at its accomplishment. This is expedient for you.
2. Where there is a will, there is a way. God honors the "willing mind," and requires according to what a man has, not according to what he has not (v. 12).

CONCLUSION

An ungenerous Christian is an incomplete Christian, for he or she is lacking in a most vital Christian grace. God loves a cheerful (hilarious) giver apparently because such a person is a reflection of His own divine character.

ILLUSTRATIONS

Sacrificial giving. A pig and a chicken were walking by a church where a charity event was taking place. The pig suggested to the chicken that they each make a contribution. "Great idea!" the chicken cried. "Let's offer them ham and eggs!"

"Not so fast," the pig retorted. "For you, that's a contribution. For me, it's a total commitment."

The giving of the Macedonians was total commitment. They "first gave their own selves to the Lord" (v. 5).

Total commitment. The story is told of a little girl who was suffering from a rare and serious disease. Her only chance of recovery appeared to be a blood transfusion from her 5-year-old brother who had survived the same disease, developing the necessary antibodies.

The doctor explained the situation to her little brother, and asked the boy if he would be willing to give his blood to his sister. After a moment of hesitation he stoically replied, "Yes, I'll do it if it will save Sis."

As the transfusion progressed, he lay in bed next to his sister and smiled, seeing the color returning to her cheeks. Then his face grew pale and his smile faded. He looked up at the doctor and asked with a trembling voice, "Will I start to die right away?" Being young, the boy had misunderstood the doctor. He thought he was going to have to give his sister all of his blood.

An Astounding Reversal

2 Corinthians 8:9

The issue under consideration in chapters 8 and 9 is the offering for the poor saints in Judea. The emphasis on Christian liberality, however, immediately draws Paul's mind back to the supreme example of the grace of giving. Here is a great gospel truth taught almost incidentally.

The word "grace" is extensively used in the New Testament. This idea of kindness or favor is expanded or enlarged by emphasizing its undeserved nature (Romans 4:6, 16; 11:6; Ephesians 2:8). In this text Paul pictures two astounding reversals: the condescension of Christ, and the exaltation of mankind.

I. THE AMAZING CONDESCENSION: CHRIST—"THOUGH HE WAS RICH, . . . HE BECAME POOR."

A. Consider the riches of Christ:

1. He had coequality with God (John 1:1, 2; 10:30, 38; 14:10; 17:21; Philippians 2:6).
2. He had a creative role and power (John 1:3; 1 Corinthians 8:6; Ephesians 3:9; Colossians 1:16; Hebrews 1:1, 2).
3. He enjoyed celestial and eternal glory from the beginning (John 8:58; 17:5, 24).
4. His heavenly status was better, and His name more excellent than that of angels (Hebrews 1:4).
5. All this is but the beginning. His "riches in glory" exhaust our imaginations and are beyond our powers of comprehension.

B. He became poor "for your sakes" (v. 9).

1. Man has a great need, being "dead in trespasses and sins" (Ephesians 2:1). As *dead,* man is unable to extricate himself from this predicament.
2. God has great love for lost mankind (John 3:16; Ephesians 2:4, 5).
3. The Law alone is inadequate (Romans 8:3; Ephesians 2:15; Hebrews 7:19).
4. God's grace, with Christ as God's agent, is sufficient (John 3:16; Romans 5:8; Ephesians 2:4, 5; 1 John 3:1; 4:9, 16).
5. In Christ, God provided the reversal to the Adamic curse (Romans 5:12-19; 1 Corinthians 15:22).

C. He came to earth voluntarily.

1. He "became obedient even unto death" (Philippians 2:7, 8).

2. He affirmed: "No man taketh [my life] . . . I lay it down of myself" (John 10:11, 15, 18).
3. This is attested to by apostolic teaching (Galatians 1:4; Ephesians 5:2; Titus 2:14; 1 John 3:16).

II. THE MERCIFUL ENDOWMENT: BELIEVERS—"THROUGH HIS POVERTY MIGHT BE RICH."

A. The poverty of the sinful state:

1. We were aliens and strangers, without hope and without God (Ephesians 2:12).
2. We were perverse with corrupt minds and destitute of truth (1 Timothy 6:5).
3. We were worthy only of the wages of sin, death (Romans 6:23; Hebrews 2:2, 3).

B. The riches of the redeemed state:

1. We have the temporal blessings of assurance (Colossians 2:2; 2 Timothy 1:12; Hebrews 10:22), comfort (John 14:1, 18; 2 Corinthians 1:3; 7:6; 2 Thessalonians 2:17), hope (2 Thessalonians 2:16; Hebrews 6:18, 19; 1 Peter 1:3), joy (Acts 8:5-8, 39; Romans 5:11; 2 Corinthians 7:4), peace (Luke 2:14; John 14:27; 16:33; Romans 5:1; 8:6; 14:17; 1 Corinthians 7:15), and rest (Matthew 11:29; Hebrews 4:3).
2. We have a spiritual inheritance now that we are heirs of God (Romans 8:17), heirs of grace (1 Peter 3:7), heirs of salvation (Hebrews 1:14), heirs of righteousness (Hebrews 11:7), and heirs of the kingdom (James 2:5).

CONCLUSION

"O the depth of the riches both of the wisdom and knowledge of God! how unsearchable are his judgments, and his ways past finding out!" (Romans 11:33). "May [you] be able to comprehend with all saints what is the breadth, and length, and depth, and height; and to know the love of Christ, which passeth knowledge, that ye might be filled with all the fulness of God" (Ephesians 3:18, 19).

ILLUSTRATION

Remarkable transformation. A boy and his father from an isolated mountain community were visiting a mall in the city for the first time. They were amazed by two shiny, silver walls that could move apart and then slide back together again. Having never seen an elevator before, they watched with interest as a rather heavy, not too attractive, older lady walked through the moving walls and into the small room beyond them. The doors closed, and the man and boy patiently waited for them to reopen. A few minutes later, the moment arrived. To their utter astonishment, a beautiful young woman stepped out. The father said quietly to his son, "Go get your mother."

The transformation they imagined was remarkable. Yet how much more remarkable is the transformation of a corrupt sinner into a child of God!

A Pattern for Christian Giving

2 Corinthians 9:6-15

Paul was concerned that the Corinthians be diligent about their year-old commitment to the offering for the poor Judean brethren. Without rehearsing his former exhortations, he simply reminds them of some essential principles for abundant and acceptable Christian giving.

I. THE RULE OF CHRISTIAN GIVING: "HE WHO SOWETH SPARINGLY SHALL REAP SPARINGLY; AND HE WHO SOWETH BOUNTIFULLY SHALL REAP ALSO BOUNTIFULLY" (v. 6).

A. This is a principle taken from nature. Among an agricultural or horticultural people this principle required no elaboration.

1. This same principle was taught in the wisdom literature of the Old Testament (Proverbs 11:24, 25; 19:17).
2. It was taught by Jesus during His earthly ministry (Luke 6:38).

B. The apostle wants the Corinthians to know that unselfish giving is not a one-way transaction—there is a God-ordained reciprocity.

II. THE STRATEGY OF CHRISTIAN GIVING: "EVERY MAN ACCORDING AS HE PURPOSETH IN HIS HEART, LET HIM GIVE, NOT GRUDGINGLY, NOR OF NECESSITY; FOR GOD LOVETH A CHEERFUL GIVER" (v. 7).

A. It must be personal and deliberate—"as he purposeth in his heart." The "heart" is the seat of all judgment, so the act of giving must be a well-reasoned decision.

B. It must be voluntary—"not grudgingly, or of necessity." A grudging gift is doing something that is alien to the true self. "Necessity" connotes a compulsion from without, whereas the Christian's compulsion should be love.

C. Christian giving is a means of identifying with God who is the first and greatest giver. God loves those who endeavor to imitate Him, being "a cheerful [literally, 'hilarious'] giver."

III. THE FOUNTAINHEAD OF CHRISTIAN GIVING: "GOD IS ABLE TO MAKE ALL GRACE ABOUND . . . HAVING ALL SUFFICIENCY

IN ALL THINGS, [THAT YE] MAY ABOUND TO EVERY GOOD WORK" (v. 8).

A. Generous giving for those in strained circumstances may appear to be foolhardy, but all misgivings fade away in the glow of God's abundant grace.

1. God is the ultimate source of all our revenues, whether great or small.
2. Where a generous spirit exists, God will provide the means for its expression.

B. Note Paul's expansiveness: "all grace . . . all sufficiency . . . all things . . . every good work." He expresses the same confidence to the Philippians "My God shall supply all your need according to his riches in glory by Christ Jesus" (4:19).

C. From this divine bounty the sincere steward will always have the sufficiency to meet all the demands made upon his or her generosity. The promise voiced through Malachi is still true: "Bring ye all the tithes into the storehouse, that there may be meat in mine house, and prove me now herewith, saith the LORD of hosts, if I will not open you the windows of heaven, and pour you out a blessing, that there shall not be room enough to receive it" (3:10).

IV. THE ASSURED RESULTS OF CHRISTIAN GIVING

A. The immediate result was the relief given to the needy brethren in Judea.

1. This was a responsibility of brotherhood and a duty of debt. It was a practical and effective means of expressing the bonds of brotherhood. The apostle John spoke to this fact: "Hereby perceive we the love of God, because he laid down his life for us: and we ought to lay down our lives for the brethren" (1 John 3:16).
2. To the Romans, Paul speaks of this duty of debt. "Indeed they owe it to them. For if the Gentiles have shared in the Jews' spiritual blessings, they owe it to the Jews to share with them their material blessings" (15:27, NIV).

B. But there is a more important result: it not only brought a blessing to the wanting brethren in Judea, but it had two more significant results.

1. It redounded to the honor and acceptance of the givers—it ratified their Christian profession. No doubt the Jerusalem church, being Jewish, was still somewhat suspicious of the validity of Gentile Christianity. This generous act of love and fellowship went far to seal the bonds of brotherhood.
2. It brought praise and thanksgiving to God. It was in keeping with the dictum of Jesus: "Let your light so shine before men, that they may see your good works, and glorify your Father which is in heaven" (Matthew 5:16). Marvelous thought indeed, that we can do something which will glorify God and turn the thoughts and hearts of others to Him!

ILLUSTRATION

Twofold result of giving. One of the most famous lines of Shakespeare's *The Merchant of Venice* speaks of the benefits of giving. "The quality of mercy is not strain'd. It droppeth as the gentle rain from heaven upon the place beneath. It is twice blest; It blesseth him that gives and him that takes" (Act 4, Scene 1).

Dealing With False Charges

2 Corinthians 10:1-18

The burden of the last chapters of 2 Corinthians is Paul's defense against false accusations. The identity of his accusers and the nature of their charges must be extrapolated from Paul's answers—much like reconstructing a telephone conversation from hearing only one side. It is quite evident that these detractors were questioning Paul's apostolic standing and authority. To this end they were taking advantage of his absence to undermine his influence. Note some of their charges and Paul's responses to them.

I. HIS LETTERS ARE BOLD, BUT HIS PRESENCE IS BASE (vv. 1, 10).

A. The intent of this accusation is to downplay, denigrate, disparage Paul and his ministry—to make him ineffective, a nobody.

1. The word translated "base" *(tapeinos)* is given various meanings: weak, lowly, mean, humble, meek, timid, fearful, cringing, wishy-washy, etc.—all with a negative or derogatory thrust.
2. They charge that his letters are terrifyingly "weighty and powerful; but his bodily presence is weak, and his speech contemptible" (v. 10). The falsity of this charge is obvious when we examine the effect of Paul's speech upon the Lycaonians (Acts 14:11, 12), upon the Jerusalem mob (Acts 22), upon Governors Felix and Festus (Acts 24, 25), and upon King Agrippa (Acts 26).

B. Paul gives an answer to this criticism.

1. His initial response is an appeal, a "beseeching," "by the meekness and gentleness of Christ" (v. 1) lest he be forced to "be bold" (v. 2) when he returns to Corinth. In this appeal he uses two words of great significance. The first word *(prautes),* signifying "mildness" or "meekness," is an inward virtue—a disposition to take no offense. It signifies that he is not speaking from any personal anger, but with the strong compassion of Christ himself. The second word *(epieikeia),* signifying "gentleness" or "clemency," is a graceful attitude—an attitude in which justice is tempered with mercy. This "sweet reasonableness" is always the appropriate Christian approach to the solution of interpersonal problems.
2. His further response is that he does have, and can exercise, apostolic authority—and will do so, if necessary, upon his impending visit. He will be as bold in presence as in writing (vv. 6, 11).

II. HE WALKS ACCORDING TO THE FLESH (v. 3).

A. This charge is that Paul is motivated by carnal interests rather than by lofty spiritual aims—that his motivation is no higher than that of carnal men.

B. He responds that he does indeed walk "in the flesh," but not "after the flesh."

1. Here he uses the term "flesh" *(sarx)* in two senses—the physical and the carnal. "In the flesh" is the inescapable human condition, man's natural physical state. Paul, like all other men, lives in a physical body. "According to the flesh" indicates subjection to the carnal, or fallen, nature. Paul declares his liberation from carnality; his aims are not dictated by fleshly appetites; his motivation comes from a supra-mundane source.
2. The evidence of his heavenly motivation and direction is that his weapons of warfare are not carnal (fleshly), but "mighty through [from] God" to destroy the strongholds of error and resistance to God (vv. 4, 5). This is not accomplished by human cleverness, but by the Spirit of God.

III. HE EXCEEDS HIS RIGHTFUL BOUNDS AND BOASTS HIMSELF OF OTHERS' LABORS (vv. 13-15).

A. They are intimating that Paul is an intruder in Corinth—that he has no priority there. They are claiming that right for themselves.

B. In answer, Paul notes that he was the first to carry the gospel to Corinth, that his accomplishments, and their own conversion, attest to his apostleship. (He had argued likewise in 1 Corinthians 9:1, 2).

1. He challenges his critics to "look deeper" and to grant him, at the very least, an equality with themselves (v. 7).
2. Then, despite his aversion to "boasting," he expands upon his labors and aims: (1) he labors for edification, not destruction (v. 8); (2) he has a higher standard of evaluation (v. 12); (3) he limits himself to God's assignment (v. 13); (4) he seeks their maturity and involvement in an expanding mission (vv. 15, 16); (5) his "glorying" is in the Lord, not in personal achievement (v. 17).

CONCLUSION

Paul's attitude toward, and concern for, his critics conformed to the standard set by Jesus in Matthew 5:44. He not only practiced this rule, but he taught it to his followers (Ephesians 4:32; Colossians 3:13). As Alexander Pope said, "To err is human, to forgive divine."

ILLUSTRATION

Unfair criticism. A wit has quipped, "Before you criticize others, you should walk a mile in their shoes. That way, when you criticize them, you are a mile away from them, and you have their shoes." It is not difficult to see that same cowardly attitude in Paul's critics at Corinth.

Glory in the Lord

2 Corinthians 10:17, 18

In our text, the apostle is quoting or alluding to Jeremiah 9:23, 24, "Thus saith the LORD, Let not the wise man glory in his wisdom, neither let the mighty man glory in his might, let not the rich man glory in his riches: but let him that glorieth glory in this, that he understandeth and knoweth me, that I am the LORD."

I. THE APPROPRIATENESS OF THE QUOTATION

A. Paul was a Jewish scholar, well acquainted with the Old Testament Scriptures. Why did he invoke this particular passage in his dealing with the Corinthians? Could it be because of the similarity between Jeremiah's situation and his own?

B. Jeremiah was speaking from a heart burdened with the spiritual apostasy of Israel. The entire ninth chapter is a great lament over the sins of his people:

1. "They be all adulterers, an assembly of treacherous men" (v. 2).
2. "They bend their tongues like their bow for lies" (v. 3).
3. "They proceed from evil to evil, and they know not me [God]" (v. 3).
4. "They will deceive every one his neighbor, and will not speak the truth" (v. 5).

C. And those were but a part of God's charges against this people! As a prophet it is Jeremiah's painful duty to declare the judgment of God upon such evil. God asks, "Shall I not visit them for these things? . . . shall not my soul be avenged on such a nation as this?" (v. 9).

1. "I will make Jerusalem heaps . . . I will make the cities of Judah desolate" (v. 11).
2. "I will feed them . . . wormwood, and give them water of gall to drink" (v. 15).
3. "I will scatter them also among the heathen, . . . and I will send a sword after them, till I have consumed them" (v. 16).

D. What a woeful fate! And why? Because in their pride and boastful self-sufficiency they deny the need of God. But God's answer through Jeremiah is: "Let him that glorieth glory in this, that he understandeth and knoweth me" (v. 24).

II. THE APPLICATION TO THE CORINTHIANS

A. Likewise, Paul is speaking from a burdened heart. His great love for the Corinthians is wounded by their arrogant self-sufficiency. Throughout the Corinthian correspondence he has to deal with human pride.

1. In the first chapter of 1 Corinthians, the apostle feels the necessity to

reprove their conduct and to remind them that "the foolishness of God is wiser than man's wisdom" (v. 25, NIV).

2. This folly is shown in that practically the whole of the epistle is spent upon problems within the Corinthian church. These included: disunity, partisan loyalties, and vanity (1 Corinthians 1–4); tolerance of immorality "such as is not so much as named among the Gentiles" (1 Corinthians 5:1); litigation against brethren in heathen court (1 Corinthians 6); marriage abuses and domestic problems (1 Corinthians 7); confusion concerning idol worship and eating meat (1 Corinthians 8); disregard for the apostolic leadership of Paul (1 Corinthians 9); abuses in public worship (1 Corinthians 10, 11); and false understanding of spiritual gifts (1 Corinthians 12–14).
3. Is this a record about which to boast? Paul answers with his first quoting of Jeremiah: "He that glorieth, let him glory in the Lord" (10:17).

B. Their character had improved little by the time of this second letter!

1. They were quick to charge Paul with fickleness (2 Corinthians 1).
2. They had been slow to deal with the incest in the church (2 Corinthians 2).
3. They were yoking unequally with unbelievers (2 Corinthians 6).
4. They had neglected the offering for the Judean brethren (2 Corinthians 8, 9).

C. By "measuring themselves by themselves" they saw no evil in themselves. Paul had to remind them that it is "not he that commendeth himself [that] is approved, but whom the Lord commendeth" (10:18). Again he alluded to Jeremiah: "Let him that glorieth glory in the Lord" (v. 24).

CONCLUSION

The first step toward recovery from our fallen state is the recognition that we have nothing of which to boast—that apart from God we are as nothing, but with God we have everything (1 Corinthians 3:21-23). Boasting is an expression of pride, and pride is one of the seven deadly sins. "Pride goeth before destruction, and a haughty spirit before a fall" (Proverbs 16:18).

ILLUSTRATION

Apostasy today. Joe Wright of Central Christian Church in Wichita opened a session of the Kansas Senate with these confessions:

We have ridiculed the absolute truth of your Word and called it pluralism; we have worshiped other gods and called it multiculturalism; we have endorsed perversion and called it an alternative lifestyle; we have exploited the poor and called it the lottery; we have neglected the needy and called it self-preservation; we have rewarded laziness and called it welfare; we have killed our unborn and called it choice; we have shot abortionists and called it justifiable; we have neglected to discipline our children and called it building self-esteem; we have abused power and called it political savvy; we have coveted our neighbor's possessions and called it ambition; we have polluted the air with profanity and pornography and called it freedom of expression; we have ridiculed the time-honored values of our forefathers and called it enlightenment.

Facing Apostasy

2 Corinthians 11:1-15

In this section of 2 Corinthians the specter of apostasy looms large, and Paul's concern for both the Corinthians and his critics is evident. Why is he so concerned? Because they are a part of the bride of Christ. In Jewish culture the "friend of the bridegroom" had many responsibilities, but the most important was to guarantee the chastity of the bride. Paul sees himself as such a "friend" and is zealous for the purity of the Corinthian church.

I. THE ISSUE OF CONCERN: IMMINENT APOSTASY

A. "I fear . . . your minds . . . be corrupted from the simplicity that is in Christ" (v. 3).

B. Corruption of doctrine and departure from the faith has always been a major problem in the relationship between God and humankind.

1. It began in the Garden of Eden and constituted a running theme all through the Old Testament (Deuteronomy 13:5; Isaiah 9:16; Jeremiah 2:8; 14:14; 23:16; Ezekiel 13:6; 28:18; Micah 3:5; Zephaniah 3:4; Zechariah 13:2, 3).
2. Jesus continued the warnings: "Beware of false prophets" (Matthew 7:15); "Many false prophets shall rise, and shall deceive many" (Matthew 24:11); "False Christs and false prophets shall rise . . . to seduce, if it were possible . . . even the elect" (Mark 13:22).

C. The problem must have been pronounced in Corinth to elicit so much concern from the apostle.

1. In 1 Corinthians he had lamented their carnality and factionalism (3:1-4), and their unbrotherly litigation against each other (6:5-8).
2. In 2 Corinthians 2:17 he spoke of "many who corrupt the word of God," and in 4:2 he alludes to some who "walk in craftiness," and "handle the word of God deceitfully."
3. In this section (or letter) he employs sharp terms for those he is combating: "super-apostles" (v. 5, NIV), "false apostles, deceitful workers, transforming themselves into apostles of Christ. . . . for Satan himself is transformed into an angel of light" (vv. 13, 14).

II. THE AGENTS OF APOSTASY: FALSE TEACHERS

A. "He that cometh preacheth another Jesus" (v. 4).

B. The original: The devil has been a corrupter of mankind from the beginning.
1. His first appearance was in the Garden of Eden to tempt Eve (Genesis 3).
2. He roams the earth (Job 1:7) "seeking whom he may devour" (1 Peter 5:8).
3. He spares no one, not even the Christ, the Son of God (Matthew 4:1-11).

C. The perennial: In every age apostates are enlisted in the devil's schemes. Throughout human history men have been his minions, some willingly (John 8:44; Acts 13:10; 1 John 3:8, 10), and some unwittingly (Matthew 13:38; 16:23).

D. The contemporary: atheism, humanism, secularism
1. Secular education argues that no thinking person can really believe in God, that Christianity is irrational and irrelevant to the thinking person.
2. A denial of God has resulted in the "dumbing down" of ethics. Even in our highest offices the message is that morality doesn't count.

E. Paul declares the exclusiveness of the gospel. His declaration in verse 4 is reiterated in Galatians 1:7-9. There is no other gospel, and let those who preach another be accursed!

III. THE METHOD OF APOSTASY: SUBTILTY, DECEIT

A. "As the serpent beguiled Eve through his subtilty" (v. 3).

B. Subtilty, cunning, deceitfulness were the most distinguishing characteristic of Satan (Genesis 3:1).
1. He deceived Eve by discrediting God and making enticing but false promises to her (Genesis 3:4, 5).
2. He is a congenital liar, and those who oppose God and deceive His people are his children (John 8:44).
3. His minions are described in frightful terms: "Their throat is an open sepulcher; with their tongues they have used deceit; the poison of asps is under their lips" (Romans 3:13).

C. Warnings against apostasy are too numerous to list in their entirety.
1. "The time will come . . . not endure sound doctrine . . . having itching ears . . . turn from the truth to fables" (2 Timothy 4:3, 4).
2. "Take heed, brethren, lest there be in any of you an evil heart of unbelief, in departing from the living God" (Hebrews 3:12).
3. "Beware lest ye also, [be] led away with the error of the wicked" (2 Peter 3:17).

ILLUSTRATION

The price of deceit. A man hit by a car in New York City in 1977 got up uninjured, but laid himself back down in front of the car, pretending he was hurt so he could collect insurance money. The car then rolled forward and crushed him to death. Paul's warning against deceit is strong because he knew that its price can be high.

Paul Vindicates His Apostleship

2 Corinthians 11:16-30

In chapter 11, Paul is being forced to engage in an exchange which is thoroughly distasteful to him, but is a matter of self-defense and of his apostleship. He has already marked his opponents in Corinth as deceivers (vv. 3, 4), as self-appointed apostles (v. 5), as pretenders (v. 13), and as minions of Satan (v. 14). All serious, but justifiable charges. He admits (v. 17) that he is resorting to uninspired tactics, and is a "fool" for doing so, but he is forced to fight fire with fire (v. 18). Now he uses a bit of irony to point out to the "wise" (v. 19) Corinthians their own folly in suffering abuses from these false apostles.

I. WHAT ARE SOME OF THESE ABUSES? (v. 20).

A. A false apostle will "bring you into bondage."

1. Their attempt was to bring the Corinthians under the Jewish Law. The same word *(katadoulo)* is used in Galatians 2:4 of "false brethren" attempting to bring the Galatian Christians "into bondage."
2. This form of "bondage" was deplored in apostolic teaching (Acts 15:7-10; Galatians 2:4; 4:24; 5:1; 2 Peter 2:19).

B. A false apostle will "devour you."

1. The same word *(katasthia)* is used in Luke 20:47 where Jesus describes the scribes as those who "devour widows' houses."
2. This charge is further enlightened by the comment "take [advantage] of you." This word refers to catching fish in a net (Luke 5:5).

C. A false apostle will "exalt himself."

1. A self-assumed authority is always more arrogant than a bona fide one. False apostles mask their inferiority with braggadocio.
2. Jewish tradition attached a greater respect to a teacher than to a parent, and these false teachers were taking advantage of it.

D. A false apostle will "smite you on the face."

1. This could refer to belittling or insulting words.
2. This could be meant quite literally (1 Kings 22:24; Luke 22:64; Acts 23:2).

II. PAUL MATCHED THE CLAIMS OF THE FALSE TEACHERS (vv. 21, 22).

A. They boasted that they were Hebrews.

1. This was a claim to undiluted stock. Jews of the *Diaspora* adopted foreign languages and customs, and the Palestinian Jews looked down upon them.
2. This claim was probably a snide dig at Paul who was born outside of Palestine and was a Roman citizen.
3. Paul countered that he was a genuine Hebrew. In fact, he had a pedigree which none of his critics could match (Philippians 3:4-6).

B. They proudly claimed to be Israelites.

1. Jacob (Israel) was the chosen progenitor, and his twelve sons were the heads of the twelve tribes—God's own people.
2. The watch-cry of Israel was, "Hear, O Israel, the LORD our God is one LORD" (Deuteronomy 6:4). They felt Paul had never been a part of this select community.
3. Paul's answer: "So am I." In fact, he was a devoted member of "the most strictest sect of our religion" (Acts 26:5).

C. Their ultimate boast was that they were "the seed [descendants] of Abraham."

1. This entitled them to the great promise that God made to Abraham long before the Law was promulgated (Genesis 12:1-3).
2. Paul, as a second-rate Jew, even a foreigner, had no claim upon this noble heritage.
3. Paul responded, "I am not only a true Israelite, the royal family of Abraham, but also of the tribe of Benjamin, the most favored and most militant of all the tribes" (Philippians 3:5).

D. They smugly boasted of being "ministers of Christ" (v. 23).

1. The insinuation here is that Paul is not a true minister of Christ.
2. Paul, as a "fool," fully rejected this claim, and went one better: "I am more!" Then he proceeded to vindicate this claim.

III. PAUL JUSTIFIED THIS BOAST (vv. 23-28).

A. Paul summarized that he was "in labors more abundant, in stripes above measure, in prisons more frequently, in deaths often" (v. 23).

C. Surely, none of these self-appointed "apostles" could match such a record of trials, tribulations, and service. "Fool" or no fool, Paul had made his case!

CONCLUSION

The Christian's defense against the calumnies of the world is the quality of one's character. If it stands the test, one needs no other defense. Paul measured up!

ILLUSTRATION

Determining genuineness. Cervantes, in *Don Quixote,* says, "The proof of the pudding is in the eating." The genuineness of anything is determined by testing.

Paul's Thorn and God's Grace

2 Corinthians 12:1-10

This entire section of 2 Corinthians, including chapters 10–13, is an apology—a defense of Paul's apostolic ministry. The accusations of his critics in Corinth have forced him, against his will, to "boast" which he calls "foolishness" (11:1, 17, 21, 23; 12:6, 11). In this passage, the apostle speaks of a most personal and mystic experience. Though hesitant to do so, he feels that he must speak of it as evidence of his genuineness. This is an experience unmatched by any of his critics. He speaks of being "caught up into paradise" (v. 4), which carries a special connotation. "Paradise" is a Persian concept—a "walled city" where kings and powerful figures shared intimate fellowship with especially cherished friends. Concerning the "surpassing nature" of this experience it "was not lawful for a man to speak." Then, lest he be tempted to an undue pride, he was given "a thorn *(skolops*—"stake") in the flesh"—"a messenger of Satan to buffet" him. (v. 7). There has been much speculation concerning the nature of this "thorn" or "stake."

I. THEORIES CONCERNING PAUL'S THORN IN THE FLESH

A. Views of prominent religious leaders

1. The Roman Catholic view: carnal temptation. This is not surprising, since this was one of the greatest problems in monastic life. The sexual temptations common in the monastery are projected on to Paul.
2. John Calvin's view: spiritual temptations. Calvin speculated that Paul's thorn was the temptation to doubt, to shirk spiritual duties, to be presumptuous, to be pretentious with respect to faith, etc.
3. Martin Luther's view: external opposition and persecution. Paul had a constant battle with those who sought to discredit him and thwart his objectives.

B. The words "thorn" and "in the flesh" strongly suggest that it was some form of bodily affliction. This has given rise to various views.

1. Paul's physical appearance. The Corinthians said, "His bodily presence is weak" (10:10). From this it is assumed that he had some physical disfigurement which hindered his work. But that would not account for the pain involved.
2. A common view is that Paul was epileptic. In Galatians 4:14 Paul says that they did not reject him. The Greek word is "did not spit at me," which was the ancient method of warding off epilepsy.
3. Another theory is that he had eye trouble. This is given slight support by

Galatians 4:15 and 6:11.

4. Perhaps the most reasonable theory is that he suffered from recurrent attacks of fever which was common in the coastal regions of the Mediterranean.

C. God's answer to Paul's prayer was typical. He did not take away the problem, but provided the strength and ability to overcome it.

II. HOW GOD'S GRACE WAS SUFFICIENT FOR PAUL

A. It enabled him to overcome physical weariness. Note his list of trials (11:23-28).

B. It enabled him to bear extreme physical pain. Almost impossible to imagine "forty stripes save one," three times "beaten with rods," three shipwrecks, floating "a night and a day" in the open sea, hunger, thirst, manifold perils, etc.

C. It enabled him to meet and withstand strong human opposition. Throughout his ministry he was beset by Jewish religionists, pagan partisans, and false brethren. Yet no amount of opposition could turn him from his mission.

D. It enabled him, as this letter makes clear, to face and endure slander. This is the most insidious and hurtful of all opposition, yet Paul faced it with faith and courage. God's grace made him indifferent to the judgments of men, but concerned only for the favorable estimate of God.

CONCLUSION

Paul had come to terms with the imponderables of life: "Therefore I take pleasure in infirmities, in reproaches, in necessities, in persecutions, in distresses for Christ's sake: for when I am weak, then am I strong" (12:10). He measured up to the exhortation of Jesus: "Rejoice, and be exceeding glad, . . . for so persecuted they the prophets which were before you" (Matthew 5:12).

ILLUSTRATION

Life isn't like that! It has been observed that we will learn the following from watching movies:

• Large, loft-style apartments in New York City are well within the price range of most people—whether they are employed or not.

• Should you decide to defuse a bomb, don't worry which wire to cut. You will always choose the right one.

• It does not matter if you are heavily outnumbered in a fight involving martial arts: your enemies will wait patiently to attack you one by one by dancing around in a threatening manner until you have knocked out their predecessors.

• Most laptop computers are powerful enough to override the communications system of any invading alien society.

Paul's thorn in the flesh taught him that even Christians do not have perfect lives. Yet God's grace is sufficient to overcome their problems.